PREDATORS

PREDATORS

GREAT HUNTERS OF THE NATURAL WORLD

MALCOLM PENNY AND CAROLINE BRETT

WITH

GABY ROSLIN

SURVIVAL

EBURY PRESS
LONDON

First published 1995

1 3 5 7 9 10 8 6 4 2

Text copyright © Survival Anglia Limited 1995

First published in the United Kingdom in 1995 by
Ebury Press
Random House, 20 Vauxhall Bridge Road, London
SW1V 2SA

Random House Australia (Pty) Limited
20 Alfred Street, Milsons Point, Sydney, New South
Wales, 2061, Australia

Random House New Zealand Limited
18 Poland Road, Glenfield, Auckland 10, New Zealand

Random House South Africa (Pty) Limited
PO Box 337, Bergvlei, South Africa

Random House UK Limited Reg. No. 954009

A catalogue record for this book is available from the
British Library

ISBN: 0 09 180749 2

Editor: Margot Richardson
Design: Jerry Goldie Graphic Design
Printed and bound in Great Britain by Butler and
Tanner Ltd, Frome and London

Papers used by Ebury Press are natural recyclable
products made from wood grown in sustainable
forests.

Contents

Introduction

If, one day, you suddenly received a phone call asking, 'How would you feel about coming face to face with some of the world's most dangerous predators, in America and Africa?', what would you say? If you were then asked, 'Would you be prepared to canoe alongside killer whales and descend into to a pit of snakes?', how would you react?

Above **With the Survival crew on location in Kenya. From left to right: Clem Vallance (director), Eddie Elmhurst (sound), Gaby Roslin, Richard Crafter (photography) and Caroline Brett (producer).**

Right **At midday in Africa it was too hot to film. Back at camp, everybody took it easy, including the neighbourhood hippos.**

I received such a call. I was so excited all I could do for several minutes was dance around making war whoops. The prospect wouldn't be everyone's idea of bliss, but I couldn't possibly have said no. To be asked to present a series of Survival programmes was like a dream come true. I am fascinated by animals, and to learn more about them in their natural environment was an opportunity I could not afford to miss.

It was not simply a matter of being asked, and saying yes. First, I had to do a film test at Whipsnade Zoo. I can't remember when I had last felt so nervous. I wanted the job badly and was worried I would try too hard, and I didn't quite know what to expect. I knew I had to learn a lot of lines quickly and then say the relevant sections in various different locations. These included the tropical house with a huge snake draped around my neck, in front of the rhino enclosure, the penguin pool and the bear pit. I came away from the experience a complete wreck, convinced that I had blown any chance I might have had originally. Three days later, I was very surprised but absolutely delighted to hear that I had got the job.

When we left England to film the 'real' thing, I wondered what I had let myself in for. However, although there were some fairly hairy moments, overall the experience was thrilling.

Above **The African plains are home to some of the world's most magnificent predators: lions, cheetahs and leopards.**

I came within touching distance of killer whales, alarmingly close to a grizzly bear and watched in amazement as a snake hatched in my hands. I was astonished to find hyaenas fascinating; I had always thought they were rather grim scavengers, but by the time we left Kenya, I was intrigued by their social systems and hunting skills. I was deeply moved when I learned about the demise of the African hunting dog, and thrilled to have a close encounter with two young leopard cubs. I find these cats incredibly beautiful, and sensual too. To have a pair of youngsters play round the wheel of our vehicle and then chase each other up a nearby tree was an overwhelming treat.

The scenery of the Alaskan peninsula where we filmed the bears was stunning beyond imagination. I felt so privileged just being there and strangely at peace amidst its isolation and unspoilt beauty. The San Juan Islands off the north-west coast of America were tamer by comparison, but islands always have a magic all of their own. The Arizona desert has the lure of the arid wilderness. The baking heat, huge unpopulated landscapes with red rock canyons, badlands and weird cactuses have an almost lunar appeal.

For me, however, nothing compares with East Africa. My grandfather lives in Zimbabwe so I have been lucky enough to visit that country on many occasions. I have come to love the vast open grasslands, scrub savannah and foothills. What makes it particularly special is its wildlife. The vast herds of antelope and zebra are staggering. The big predatory cats are awe-inspiring. It is impossible not to withdraw from a deep-rooted sense of fear, yet at the same time be drawn by their magnificence and power. I have to keep pinching myself to come down from cloud nine and to remind myself that what seems like a blissful dream is all real.

I am also reminded, almost daily, that these wildlife and wilderness spectaculars may not last much longer. These days, there is much depressing news about wildlife and the environment. Television, the press and literature bombard us with endless tales of doom and gloom and of species facing extinction. I find the problems of over-population, poverty and habitat destruction terrifying – and that is only scratching the surface of our global dilemmas.

The world is our children's heritage and it is worth saving for them. I believe that where there is a will there is a way, and that there is hope. But it is up to us – all of us.

Above **We were lucky enough to have William Chepkwony on our team. He is reputedly one of the best guides in the Maasai Mara game park in Kenya, and could spot predators that all the rest of us missed**

Gaby Roslin

1
Lions

Queen of the Predators

The lion is always thought of as the king of the beasts, proud and dominant, the greatest predator of the African plains. With his majestic maned head and arrogant manner, he certainly looks the part. However, recent research has resulted in a new understanding of the lion's way of life, showing that a pride of lions is led by females, that they are the monarchs of all they survey, and that the male is an essential but only temporary element in the life of a lioness's family.

Left **Lions spend up to twenty hours a day sleeping and resting. After gorging themselves on a kill, they can lie around for up to three days while they digest their huge meal.**

A Tonne of Meat

A pride of lions hunting is a dramatic sight. The females, their golden coats blending perfectly with the dry grass of the African plains, seem in no hurry as they walk purposefully towards their intended prey, perhaps a herd of zebra or a group of buffalo. As the prey becomes jittery, aware of the approaching predators, the lions fan out to encircle the herd and cut off their lines of retreat. One or two of them stand up in full view, attracting the attention of the prey, while the others lie flat, invisible, on the other side of the herd. With luck, the herd moves away from the lions they can see, straight into the ambush laid by the rest of the pride. The lionesses select likely victims, and close in, ignoring the rest of the herd. Clinging on with sharp, hooked claws and using their weight and strength, one or

Below **Lions often kill large animals by suffocation. Clamping its jaws over the victim's mouth and nose, the lion shuts off its prey's air supply.**

two of them drag their victim to the ground. Small prey is killed by a bite to the back of the neck, which severs the spinal column. Larger animals are suffocated: one or more of the lionesses close their jaws round the victim's throat, clamping off its air. Soon, the hunt is over, and the whole pride settles down to feed together.

Hunting in this way, as few as three or four lions can pull down a buffalo weighing more than a tonne. This is plenty of food for all the hunters and their young, as well as for the lordly males who rush in after the hunt to take first choice of the food.

Each adult lion needs about 5kg (11lb) of food per day throughout the year to stay alive. If the pride can kill large prey, it only needs to hunt every ten days or so to provide enough food for all its members. A shortage of prey, or too much attention from scavengers such as hyaenas, makes life more difficult. When food is short, the first to suffer are the cubs, who will be prevented from feeding until the males have had their fill. The females are next in line; if there is none left when the males have eaten, both the females and cubs starve. There is evidently a limit to the teamwork of the pride. The apparent contradiction between selfless sharing and callous disregard has been a puzzle for years, but recent research is finally beginning to unravel the complex life of the pride.

The Family Cat

The lion is unique as the only species of wild cat that lives in multi-sex groups. Why this should be so was a mystery, until it became possible to identify lions individually on sight. Each lion has a pattern of spots round the muzzle, among its whiskers, that is unique to the individual and unchanging through life. As soon as researchers realised this, they could begin to understand the true structure of the pride, and with it the secrets of the lions' family life.

A typical pride consists of three to fifteen resident females with their cubs, and two or three males. The lionesses are all related by birth: they can be grandmother, mother, daughter, sister, cousin or aunt of the others. The males are not related to the females, but they can be each other's brothers or cousins. On the other hand, they may be quite unrelated: friends who

met in the bush. Pairs and trios of males are just as often unrelated as related. Groups of four or more are usually males from the same pride.

The pride defends an exclusive territory which may be anything from 35 to 350 sq km (13.5 to 135 sq miles), depending on the abundance of prey in the area. In the Serengeti, in Tanzania, where prey is plentiful, a typical territory is 65 sq km (25 sq miles); but in Etosha, in Namibia, where prey is less abundant, territories may be five times the size.

The territory is defended by the whole pride. The males patrol its boundaries regularly, spraying strongly scented urine and roaring loudly. The scent lingers for days, and the roars can be heard from a long way away, so that there is no chance of accidental invasion by lions from outside. Males defend the pride territory from rival males, while females defend it from other females and males.

The only time unrelated females have been known to join forces is in the Kalahari desert. The conditions are so harsh in the area that adult lionesses cannot afford to allow all their female offspring to stay in the

*Left **The awe and majesty of the king of the beasts has inspired poets, artists and writers for centuries, and lions are still one of the most captivating of all predators.***

*Below **Working as a team, lions are able to bring down prey as large as buffalo. Three lions cannot finish the whole carcass, so there will be plenty left for the hyaenas waiting to clean up afterwards.***

pride's territory. Young females wandering alone or in pairs will then join with other solitary females. Just like related females, they do this mainly to defend their territory, cubs and kills from other lions, but also hyaenas. Many researchers now think that hyaenas were one of the main reasons lions banded together in the first place. Solitary lions can lose so many kills to gangs of hyaenas that they can die of starvation. It seems more important for lions to band together to defend their homes, food supply and mates than to work as a team to catch food.

Within the territory, the lionesses hunt and rear their cubs in an atmosphere of peace and co-operation, watched over by the affectionate and tolerant males. The cubs seem able to take amazing liberties with their adult relations, climbing over them and biting their tails between bouts of wrestling and mock hunts, in which they stalk each other – and often the adults – then pounce and bite. As they grow, they range further from the resting pride, exploring their territory and experimenting with whatever they find. They chase anything that moves, like all young cats. Starting with feathers and leaves blown in the wind, they graduate to birds or mice, and move on to larger and more active animals. This can lead them into danger. Fearless as they are, they seem to expect other adult animals to be as tolerant as their extended family. In one unlucky episode, three cubs were found dead, gored to death by a warthog they had been playfully trying to catch.

Lions spend about nineteen hours a day resting, the adults sprawling in the shade while the cubs play round them. A pride at rest, after a hunt, is the image of contentment and stability; but its calm can easily be disturbed from outside, where violence and bitter rivalry are never far away.

An Extended Family

All the lionesses were born into the pride, so they are closely related in the female line. Their cubs all have a very similar genetic make-up, so an aunt who hunts to feed her nephews and nieces is helping to pass into the next generation a set of genes very like those of her own offspring. Lions take this co-operation a step further than any other mammal: females will suckle any cub in the pride, whether or not it is her own. The cubs know which

Above **Lion cubs' spots help to conceal them from enemies during the first few weeks of life. As the cubs get older and join their mother's pride out on the open plains, they lose their markings so that they too can blend in with the golden grass of their new surroundings.**

female is producing the most milk at any given time, and will go to her to feed, leaving the less productive females in peace. It is not uncommon to see two or three cubs of very different ages and sizes feeding from the same contented female.

The advantages of this are obvious, from the point of view of the females in the pride. If one of them should become sick or injured, her cubs will be looked after until she recovers, because they represent more than just her personal contribution to the next generation. Similarly, she will hunt and lactate, and share her prey and her milk, to support the cubs of

*Overleaf **While the adult members of the pride go out to hunt, any cubs not old enough to join them are often left in a hideaway, such as a rocky outcrop, where they will be relatively safe.***

GABY:
COOL CATS

Cats do not have a lot of sweat glands in their skin. They cannot cool down in the same way we can, by perspiring.

However, anyone who has taken a pet cat to a vet will know that they do have sweat glands in their paws. A nervous cat sweats and damp paw prints all over the vet's examination table. An over-heated cat will also pant like a dog to lose heat by the evaporation of saliva from its tongue.

Cats, unlike dogs, also have a special arrangement to cool their brains. This is important because if a mammal overheats and hot blood rushes to the brain, it will pass out. Blood cooled in the nasal passages travels to the base of the brain. There it cools blood in the arteries that supply the brain. The system is most important when a cat is hunting. The animal soon warms up with the exertion and it cannot afford to faint mid-pounce.

Cats can also cool off by lying in ponds, pools or rivers, but most of them hate water. The jaguar is a notable exception. It is often found at midday, lying in a river. Leopards will cross rivers and lakes, but very large areas of water are a barrier to them.

Above **A young lion growls at its own reflection in a pool, taken by surprise when it arrives to drink.**

any of her relatives in the pride, as if they were her own. Another less-obvious advantage is that by taking the milk of all the females in the pride, the cubs may acquire a wider range of antibodies, and thus better protection against disease, than if they were fed only by their own mothers.

The researchers discovered that the position of the males in this idyllic family life is short-lived and much less secure. The lionesses own the territory, while the lions are temporary visitors, employed as guardians and fathers, but only for as long as they have the strength to hold their positions.

Invaders

The male lions in a pride are also usually related, having grown up together in another pride until they were expelled, usually by the arrival of a new group of stepfathers. Having roamed the plains for a year or two, hunting as best they could, they took over a pride for themselves by ousting the resident males in a territorial battle. Now their job is to hold their new territory for as long as they can, fathering as many cubs as possible, and benefiting from the handsome supply of food provided by the lionesses.

The phrase 'the lion's share' is a good description of the way food is divided among the pride after a kill. To us humans, it seems as if the mother lions are falling down in their duty to their cubs by letting the males take the best of the food until they are satisfied, then feeding themselves, and leaving the cubs until last. This is to misunderstand the value of the lions to the lionesses, the mistresses of the pride.

The greatest danger to the cubs in a pride is invasion by strange males. The only way for females to protect their cubs from this deadly threat is to make sure that they have some strong males in residence, to fight for them while the cubs grow up. If the price of keeping these males in peak condition is to go short of food from time to time, even at the cost of a sickly cub or two, it is a price worth paying.

For two years, or sometimes a little more, the system works. The males keep the borders of the territory secure, so that the cubs can grow in safety. The males evidently enjoy fatherhood, playing gently with the cubs even when they are at their most boisterous, patrolling conscientiously and fighting fiercely for as long as they can. After all, they are passing their

own genes down into the next generation, just as much as the females. There is occasional jealousy between the males, when they compete for the favours of one of the females that has come into season. They fight over her, but it is only a mock battle: as fellow members of the same team, they can't afford to risk wounding each other. Life seems peaceful and stable; but eventually a couple of strange males will come from outside the pride, too young and fit for the residents to repel, and their idyll will be over.

Infanticide

Battles for territory can be extremely violent, sometimes resulting in the death of the loser, but usually they are more tactical, a show of strength in

Above **Zoo lions are fed about 7kg (16lb) of meat daily. In the wild, lions cannot rely on one 'square meal' each day, so they eat as much as they can whenever possible. A male lion can consume 23kg (50lb) of meat at one sitting, which is the equivalent, taking size into consideration, of a man eating sixteen steaks at a single meal.**

Right **To guard their kills from ever-present scavengers, lions often sleep next to the carcass.**

which the side that is outnumbered backs down. Even in physical conflict, lions avoid using their formidable weaponry to the full. To make a really violent attack would be to escalate the fight to the point where the opponent might fight back in desperation and cause serious harm. Instead, snarling and pawing at each other, each lion does his best to intimidate the enemy until one side gives up the contest.

The defending lions usually patrol in a group, because they know that the invaders will arrive in twos and threes. If one of them is caught alone by a team of wandering males, he will inevitably lose the conflict, and the end of his team's tenure could be in sight. It is only a matter of time before this happens.

When invaders have driven off the resident males, the lionesses initially go into hiding. The powerful young newcomers have beaten off the lionesses' defenders and friends of the last two years, after all, and they have every reason to be afraid of them.

However, the newcomers are not looking for the females at this stage, though their main motive in taking over the pride was to find mates. Their first quarry is the young cubs. They hunt them down and kill them with a bite to the neck. Sometimes they eat some or all of them, but only when the massacre is over. The instinctive human response to this is horror, but to the lions taking over the pride it is the only sensible course of action. They have only two years or a little more to sire and rear cubs of their own, and to raise some other father's offspring would be a waste of time and effort. Furthermore, the females will not come into season while they have small cubs, perhaps not for a year or more. The newcomers cannot afford to wait that long to start their own family.

The grown male cubs, those more than eighteen months old, present a different problem. The new males have no wish to share the available food with these unrelated males, but they do not want to risk fighting them, in case they get hurt themselves. Instead, they drive the young males off, by repeated threats, until they wander away, in a group, to feed themselves as best they can.

When the coast is clear, the young cubs dead and the adolescent males sent packing, the males do not have to look for the females: they come out of hiding and begin to offer themselves to the new arrivals.

Left **Lionesses usually stay in their mother's pride for life. Surrounded and supported by their mother, sisters, cousins and aunts, they are more secure and tend to live longer than their male relatives who are always forced out of the pride as adolescents.**

Overleaf **Lionesses are perfectly camouflaged against a typical background of long dry grass. They use it as cover when stalking their prey.**

The Waiting Game

In a display that to human eyes seems heartless, the lionesses who have lost young cubs flirt outrageously with the new males in their lives. They all come into season shortly after their cubs are dead and make themselves available immediately for mating. The males respond, mating repeatedly with all the lionesses in turn. At this stage they show no jealousy of each other. They patrol their new territory, learning and marking its boundaries and driving off intruders. For three months, the pride hunts, feeds and mates, in an existence that seems to be the essence of unbridled pleasure-seeking. But there is much more to it than that.

The lionesses are in charge in this situation, as in all others affecting the pride. By making life easy and pleasurable for the males, the females make sure that they will not wander off as suddenly as they arrived. By taking time to get to know them, they are forging bonds that will be important when the first cubs are born, when the males will have to exercise patience and tolerance towards all members of the pride. Above all, none of the lionesses will become pregnant during this three-month honeymoon.

Below **Lions can mate as often as once every twenty minutes, over periods of several hours, for up to four days. Mating helps males, new to a pride after a takeover, both to form bonds with the females and to reinforce the relationship during their reign over the pride.**

How this works is still unknown, but its function is clear. Until the lionesses can be sure that the new males are powerful enough to defend them and their cubs, they will not make the investment of giving birth. It is as if they want to see their new protectors prove themselves in action as effective guardians of their territory before they will produce heirs that might be summarily dispossessed.

The gestation period of a lioness is three and a half months. Almost exactly six and a half months after the new males take over the pride, several of the lionesses will give birth, and the pride will resume its idyllic existence of co-operation and affection – until the guardians are overcome in their turn by another team of wandering males.

Above **In most species of wild cat, the males and females look similar, although males are generally bigger. Lions are exceptional: only the male has a mane. The ruff of hair is designed to make its wearer appear larger and therefore more threatening to rivals.**

Wandering Males: the Pressure of Time

The adolescent males that were driven into the wilderness by the arrival of their new stepfathers are not as badly off as they might seem. Having been supplied with food by their mothers and aunts until they were forced to leave home, they are not at first very competent hunters; but hunger and the abundance of game soon combine to teach them to find enough to eat. If the young pride-mates stay together, they will form a hunting team that is perfectly able to kill prey large enough to share. If they split up, each individual is capable of killing enough small game for himself. These individuals do not stay alone for long: they soon form friendships with other male lions of about the same age that they meet during their wanderings, spending as much as two years together until they find a pride ripe for takeover. The time together replaces the bonds of their juvenile pride with bonds of another sort, forged by shared experiences and a common purpose.

All these young lions have a common drive, which is to take over a pride and sire cubs before they are too old. If they left their native pride without pressure they will be about three or four years old when they become nomads. If they were driven out by new males, they will be perhaps a year younger. By the time they are four or five years old, they will be in their prime. They cannot know it, but they usually have only another two or three years at best after this to complete the task before they become too old to fight off other challengers. (Whether they can be said to know it or not, their hormones will make sure that they take the right course of action.)

As loners, they will have little chance. Forming a team, either with their own pride-mates or with other bachelors met at a kill or a waterhole, is their best chance of success. The thing that astonished the researchers when they began to work out how the young males managed was the total lack of rivalry between them. In other species, males about to breed fight

Left **The male lion is the largest predator in Africa. Although he rarely takes part in a hunt, he uses his superior bulk and strength to feed first and secure 'the lions share'.**

off others to ensure that the forthcoming offspring are theirs alone; but with lions, living in their unique social system, the lone fighter would be doomed to remain without descendants. His only chance is to sink his selfish instincts into co-operation with others.

The wandering groups of males come under great pressure as time goes by. After two years of successful survival in the wilderness they have proved themselves as hunters, and they have learned to share their prey. They have practised fighting as a team on the rare occasions when they have to drive off other teams prospecting the same area. Eventually, they mature into full-grown adults. At this stage they start to fail more often in their hunts. They grow so large their prey find them easy to spot. A lion's huge shaggy mane may intimidate a rival male but it is a hindrance when its owner is trying to sneak up on herds of antelope. The males need females to hunt for them, and the urge to reproduce becomes too strong to resist. At every possible chance they will try to invade the territory of the nearest pride. They may fail at first, but usually they will succeed sooner or later.

GABY: LION DANCE

In the past, young Maasai warriors had to prove their worth as men by participating in a lion hunt. When they were successful, they returned to their village and in celebration performed a special lion dance. Once the whole village would have joined in, but these days the dance has lost most of its significance. Lion hunting has been made illegal. The Maasai still chase away lions but troublesome ones are trapped or tranquillised and relocated to safe areas by the wildlife authorities.

Right The Maasai still perform their tradition lion dance but nowadays it is mainly as entertainment for tourists.

The Sisterhood

For the lionesses, life is much more stable. They spend their whole lives within the same territory, among the relations that they know well. If they fall ill, or get injured during a hunt, their sisters and cousins and aunts will supply them with food and look after their cubs, and if their territory is threatened by a lone wandering male, they are powerful enough as a group to keep him out, while their current male guardians are holding the borders against the more dangerous travelling bachelor bands.

Female cubs stay within the pride, gradually taking their place as adult members, eventually becoming mothers themselves. There is no danger that they will be mated by their natural fathers, because by the time that they are mature, the lion that sired them will be long gone, displaced from the pride and probably dead.

The success of lions as a species grows from the stability of the prides, which itself arises from the long-term ownership of the territory by the group of lionesses.

Humans probably learned the harmful effects of inbreeding soon after they changed from being hunter-gatherers to farmers. Father–daughter,

Above **Large rocky outcrops, known as kopjes, provide lions with an ideal vantage point to keep a lookout for possible prey.**

Overleaf **Two lionesses lead their cubs across the dry salt-lake bed in Tanzania's Ngorongoro Crater.**

mother–son and sibling matings cause abnormalities that can be fatal. In the wild, most animals have behavioural systems that ensure against inbreeding, but it does occasionally happen. The most astonishing is in the case of the cheetah (see Chapter 6). Cheetahs are so inbred their genetic material is remarkably uniform. One of the consequences of this is that males produce extraordinarily high numbers of structurally abnormal sperm. Most of these sperm are non-viable, so the male cheetah's fertility is considerably reduced.

Inbreeding has recently been discovered in one population of lions. The Ngorongoro Crater in Tanzania is home to the highest density of lions in the world. The hundred or so lions that live in the crater rarely, if ever, leave. This is partly due to the high and steep walls to the crater, but also because prey is so abundant, the predators have little reason to hunt else-where. The result, though, has been to cause inbreeding. Researchers have found that male lions living in the crater produce twice as many abnormal sperm as those found in the neighbouring plains in the Serengeti National Park. The crater lions have less genetic diversity, increased juvenile mortality and are more susceptible to disease.

Hard Times

In many parts of the lion's habitat in Africa, there are two seasons in the year: wet and dry. During the wet season, food and water are both abundant, with plenty of grass to attract a large number of herbivores, such as wildebeest and zebra, for the lions to hunt. The truest test of the success of the pride comes during the dry season, when the grass dies down and food for lions is in short supply. The herds of wildebeest move away, and many of their predators move with them, including some of the wandering male groups. For the residents, out on the parched plains, the few remaining non-migrating animals are hard to find, and the short grass provides scant cover for hunting.

The lions are reduced to foraging for whatever meagre food they can find, and even, finally, to scavenging from the kills of other, better adapted animals. Some of the food they find is inaccessible to lions: ostrich eggs for example.

Ostriches begin to lay during the dry season, and before they start filling their communal nests, they often lay single eggs and abandon them. The lions recognise them as potential food but most cannot break into the eggs to eat them. They can pick them up, but even with their jaws at full stretch they cannot exert enough pressure to crack the sturdy shell. Only very old males, with their teeth well worn down, can sometimes manage to bring enough pressure to bear to break an ostrich egg. For the rest, the food remains tantalisingly out of reach.

During the dry season, single lions have a better chance of getting enough to eat by scavenging. One of their unwilling providers is the cheetah. Cheetahs do not need cover to hunt: they catch their prey by a short sprint, at 100km (62 miles) per hour, so the short dry grass is no handicap to them. In some ways, it makes their task easier. Unfortunately for the cheetah but fortunately for the lions, the chase is visible from far away, often as a twisting column of dust snaking across the plain. A single lion

Above **When the migrating herds of big animals have moved out of their territory, lions can come close to starvation. Then they will eat anything, even bare bones.**

can make its way towards the kill and rob the cheetah of its prey with no trouble at all.

Like other solitary hunting animals, the cheetah will not stand and fight for its prey when challenged. It simply cannot risk being injured and being unable to hunt, perhaps for several days, especially when it has cubs to feed. When it sees a lion coming, a cheetah will eat as much as it can before the lion arrives, and then take to its heels. It is estimated that lions may obtain almost 30 per cent of their food in the dry season by robbing other predators.

In the dry season, though, being in a large pride has one main advantage. Among the animals remaining resident on the plains are buffalo, large and formidable animals that are far too big and dangerous for individual lions to bring down. By co-operating in the hunt, a pride can catch and kill enough food for all its members for several days.

Surveys have shown that singles and members of large prides get about the same amount of food each. The least well fed are the groups of two or

Above **Usually, only starving males will tackle a porcupine. A quill embedded in a mouth or paw can cause a debilitating infection, reducing the lion's hunting ability.**

Right **Lions can survive for several days without water but they prefer to quench their thirst daily. As their prey frequent the same waterhole, it is often the location of a successful hunt.**

Above **Although lions can pick up an ostrich egg in their mouths, it is almost impossible for them to break the shell for its nourishing contents.**

three. They do not have enough power to bring down large animals, and they have to share such small game as they can catch.

The range of food that lions take during the dry season shows the pressure that they are under. Recorded prey includes grass mice, lizards, tortoises and quail, and even termites, locusts and snakes. Where wet-season lagoons are drying out, fish become trapped in muddy pools, and lions have been seen scooping them out for lack of anything else to eat.

Water is not a daily necessity for lions, though they will drink every day if it is available. They can go without for four or five days in times of shortage, and may even resort to chewing the shoots of plants or eating wild melons when there is no other supply. In some arid areas, lions can sur-

vive without any surface water at all, apparently by using the moisture from the stomach contents of their prey. In a really serious drought, most of the lions in an area may die, leaving large empty territories to be re-colonised when the rains return.

Team Players or Individuals?

Many scientists have studied the hunting behaviour of lions, and their conclusions have varied from a conviction that lions are co-operative hunters, with cunning strategies of ambush, to the rather dour attitude that they are individualists that just happen to hunt in groups. An account of a lioness attacking a herd of Thomson's gazelles (or Tommy) seems to suggest teamwork of a high order. It was written by J M Cullen in 1969, who described watching a lioness strolling above a swamp where a large herd of gazelles were coming down to drink.

'She appeared to take no notice of the herd until the gazelles were between her and the reed-covered swamp. The lioness then rushed forward at a terrific speed, scattering the panic-stricken Tommy in all directions. At least twenty of these little animals were chased into the reeds, where they could only move in short leaps covering very little ground. As soon as this happened other lions and lionesses and half grown cubs poked their heads up and at once ran over to the trapped gazelles. Eight Tommy were killed in less than a minute.'

This is quoted in Jonathan Kingdon's huge and magnificent book *East African Mammals,* as an example of lions 'taking advantage of the consequences of other pride members' hunting behaviour'. Kingdon goes on to conclude that lions are not truly co-operative hunters, though there is a 'tendency for individuals or groups to fall out and thus encircle prey'. Other observers would say that this encircling, and indeed the habit of observing what the other lions are doing, is the best evidence available that lions do co-operate.

One commonly reported weakness in the hunting technique of lions is that they ignore the direction of the wind and stalk their prey from wherever they happen to be. Here again, one observer's view differs from another, depending presumably on his opinion of the lion's intelligence.

Overleaf **Prey animals instinctively know when a predator is stalking. These buffalo will not run as long as they have the lion in sight.**

GABY: ELEPHANT ENCOUNTER

Late one afternoon, we were returning from filming lions. The light was stunning. On clear nights, as the sun sinks over the Maasai Mara National Park in south-west Kenya, it suffuses the whole landscape with a mellow warmth. We called this 'our special hour'; by half past six it would be all over.

That particular evening we had to go through the park gates to get back to our camp. The rangers on the gates warned us not to go our usual route home, but to take a detour because a lone bull elephant was on the rampage. Apparently, he had been charging tourist vehicles. We set off on the longer course. None of us minded: being out in Africa at this hour was heaven. We were all silent, simply soaking up the beauty of it all.

Suddenly, without any warning, there was an enraged bull elephant looming menacingly right in front of us. It is not until an African elephant is standing very close, trunk high and ears wide, that you realise just how enormous one can be. Our driver rammed the gears into reverse and backed up as fast as he could. The elephant had obviously switched its course out of sight of the rangers. It was a very 'hot-making' experience.

To my surprise, the bull did not follow us. Instead, it seemed

completely oblivious to our presence. Its eyes had a glazed look to them, almost like it had gone slightly mad or had taken a hallucinatory drug. Every few minutes or so, it would fan its ears, raise and shake its head, paw the ground to create a cloud of dust, trumpet and make a mock charge. Then it did the same thing only in a completely different direction. For all the world, it

looked as if it was having its own private battle with an invisible enemy. We backed up slowly and went home the quick way!

Later, I asked several elephant experts the reason behind this weird behaviour. One explanation offered was that the bull could have been coming into 'musth'. During this period, its male hormone levels increase. This causes, among other things, glands

Above **It is often surprising just how close people can get to lions. Due to tourism, those in national parks have accepted vehicles as part of their landscape.**

below the bull's eyes to secrete a constant trickle of fluids. To me, musth bulls look as if they are constantly weeping. They are not sad; in fact, they are more aggressive than usual. As they search for females in heat they will challenge any smaller or equal-sized male. In their agitated state, they have been know to charge at vehicles, release their aggression on trees and generally behave in a slightly strange way.

Another suggestion was that the bull could have been wounded by a Maasai spear or a poacher's bullet. In his pain and bewilderment, he could simply have been trying to take out his foe and relieve his suffering. As we saw no evidence of any wound, we all hoped that was not the reason.

Apparently, the likely interpretation was that the bull was a teenager who was simply playing. He had probably been flexing his muscles and showing off his masculinity.

We will never know if the experts were right on not. We did not hang around long enough to

Above **Like all cats, lionesses carry their cubs by the scruff of their necks. The cubs respond instinctively by going limp which reduces any risk of injury and eases their mother's task of moving them.**

One very distinguished scientist, Dr George Schaller, recorded carefully how successful lions were when they were hunting in various conditions. He found that they killed six times more often when they hunted with the wind in their face than when it was blowing their scent towards the prey, but that they did not seem to learn from their mistakes. Writing earlier, an equally celebrated naturalist, Colonel Richard Meinertzhagen, described admiringly how he had watched two lionesses lie in wait until the rest of

their pride had worked their way upwind of a herd of zebra, which panicked when they could smell them and ran straight into the jaws of the waiting pair.

The difference between these two attitudes is twenty years. The more modern view is that lions are not very clever. Perhaps there is a middle ground that might suggest that even if a pride of closely related lionesses is acting as a crowd of individuals, they might over the years begin to help each other out, or develop a certain degree of co-operation, even if only because some of them are older and more experienced than the others.

The Survival of the Lion

In the wild, lions have to overcome a number of set-backs to their population. In the Serengeti, 67 per cent of the cubs die each year from starvation, being killed by hyaenas or other predators, or by males taking over the pride. Over 5 per cent of pride females die each year, from fighting with other lions, old age or disease. The recruitment rate of new cubs into the population is more than enough to keep up the numbers. The young wandering males keep up the pressure on the older lions, making sure that the prides are well defended and that there is no room for weak or sick males in the population. Weak or sick females, on the other hand, live longer than they would if they were males, because they are looked after so well by their relatives in the prides.

The most important thing is to keep the pride intact for the benefits that it brings to all its members. Groups of related females can work together to ensure that their genes are passed on into the next generation, in the form of well-fed cubs who will grow into successful hunters in their turn.

Like all the other large African animals, lions are safe only in the national parks. Outside, they are vulnerable to the rapid increase in the human population which has proved fatal to most other wildlife. Some are killed by local farmers to protect their livestock, and others are still killed for sport, once they venture beyond the boundaries of the parks.

However, where they are protected from human pressures, lions, with their unique family life, have proved themselves mistresses of their environment: queens among predators.

Chapter 2
Snakes:
Low-level Predators

'Thou art cursed above all cattle and above every beast of the field. Upon thy belly shalt thou go, and dust shalt thou eat all the days of thy life. And I will put enmity between thee and the woman, and between thy seed and her seed: it shall bruise thy head, and thou shalt bruise his heel.'

Genesis: Chapter 3, verses 14–15

The distrust of snakes goes far back in human history, and indeed, in the evolution of the primates. Baby chimpanzees reared in captivity with no experience of snakes react with fear and loathing when they first see one. There is something about these legless reptiles, with their magical way of moving, their eerie senses and above all their venom, that sets them apart from all other predators. Perhaps the enormous number of misconceptions and old wives' tales that are associated with them also adds to our repugnance.

Left **Far from being floundering, legless beasts, snakes can move and strike with lightning speed. In addition, the spitting cobra's fangs act like water pistols and can squirt venom accurately into the eyes of its enemy from up to 4m (13ft) away.**

Legless Locomotion

To the average human, one of the most horrifying things about snakes is the way they move, gliding swiftly along without legs, wings or fins. Other unpopular creatures, such as bats or spiders, at least have limbs so that we can see how they are getting from place to place. Snakes seem supernatural, flowing and unstoppable across all kinds of terrain. Although they can strike with lightning speed, they are relatively slow over long distances. The swiftest snake is the black mamba, which can keep up with a jogging man. The hissing sand snake comes a close second. It can keep pace with a human walking briskly.

Snakes evolved from lizards, about 130 million years ago. They are the most modern reptiles, the peak of a very successful group. Theories about how they evolved vary, but the most popular is that they took refuge from competition with other reptiles by burrowing underground, in the process losing their eyes and, progressively, their limbs. Reptiles such as burrowing skinks illustrate a stage in this process, having very small legs that are incapable of carrying their body off the ground. When the competition eased, so the story goes, and when the first small mammals had appeared, to offer a new type of prey, the snakes returned to ground level. They re-evolved their eyes in a unique new design, and they brought with them the ability to move about without legs – and to alarm every primate that saw them, when at last the primates evolved in their turn.

Not all snakes have lost every trace of limbs. Constrictors and pythons have a pair of small claws that are the remains of their hind legs. Snakes have a long series of ribs, as many as four hundred of them, which support the muscles that give these reptiles their motive power. The muscles transmit their force to the ground via enlarged scales on the snake's belly, giving a grip like the tracks of a tank, so that even large, heavy snakes can flow almost vertically up tree trunks and rock faces. Over mud or leaf litter, a snake can progress effortlessly, in one continuous line. Some of the smaller species use their straight-line movement to follow their prey into holes where they would be safe from most other predators.

For swifter progress, the snakes use their grip on the ground in a different way. Instead of gliding, they throw the body into curves, which flow backwards towards the snake's tail, driven by powerful lateral muscles.

This serpentine locomotion is a remnant of their earlier reptile ancestry: lizards run in the same way, keeping a grip on the ground with their legs. In its turn, this way of moving comes from even farther back in evolution, from the way in which fish swim. Water snakes swim quickly and efficiently with this type of movement.

On loose sand, the muscles and ribs are useless because the ground moves backwards instead of the snake moving forwards. A few specialists have overcome this problem as part of their adaptation to living in deserts, by adopting a way of moving known as 'side-winding'. The curves of serpentine locomotion are raised off the ground, so that the snake touches the sand in only two places, seeming to roll across the surface, but still at only the walking pace of the average human.

*Below **To overcome the difficulty of moving over sand, vipers and rattlesnakes, which live in deserts, have evolved the method of moving called side-winding. The snake throws itself into a series of S bends and skims over the surface of the sand.***

Above **Snakes have one advantage that most predators lack: they can disarticulate their jaws. Their mouths can then open as wide as their elastic skin can stretch.**

The Impossible Swallow

The advantages of having a long, muscular body are numerous, but there are certain drawbacks, among them the problem of feeding. Other animals get wider below the head, whereas snakes are, if anything, narrower; yet, as they cannot chew, they have to swallow their prey whole. They overcome the problem by having a lower jaw that can be dislocated at will, leaving an elastic opening that leads straight to their waiting stomach.

The secret is in the quadrate bone, which in other animals is part of the fixed hinge between the upper and lower jaws. If a chewing animal such as a dog dislocates its jaw, it is unable to feed at all, since its muscles can exert no leverage on the food. A snake has teeth only for holding its prey. Once the quadrate bone has been released from its mounting, these teeth prevent the prey from escaping, while muscles lower down its body draw the victim inexorably into the ever-widening gape. When the last vestige of the prey has vanished into the darkness, the jaw is re-articulated, ready for the next bite.

GABY: SNAKE-PIT SURVIVAL

I remember my first meeting with Caroline Brett, the Survival *Predators* producer. We were having a preliminary talk about the possibilities of my involvement in the series. She looked me straight in the eye and said, 'How do you feel about standing in a pit of snakes?' I thought she was joking and said, 'No worries'. 'Good,' she said, 'because I think I can organise to get seventy snakes in a small pit at the back of a friend's house in Arizona. Oh, and by the way, none of them will be venomous.' I did not blink an eyelid. I knew she was kidding and I was not going to fall for it.

Several months later, in the fierce heat of the Arizona desert, I stood at the bottom of that pit surrounded by a mass of writhing snakes. (None of them was venomous, but some had a mean bite.) I was soon helping to put them in position around me. Everyone was concentrating hard and before I knew it, or even had time to think about it, the whole thing was over.

When it actually came to it, being in a pit of snakes was a doddle. The heat was something else, though. At midday you could burn your hand just by touching a rock.

Right **Being in a pit of snakes – even those without venom – is an experience I will never forget.**

To avoid suffocating itself as it swallows its prey, a snake has a pro-truding tube at the top of its windpipe, known as the glottis, through which it can still breathe while the rest of its mouth is crammed with food.

The Egg Trick

Eggs might be thought to present a special problem for snakes, but in fact they are the favourite food of one in particular: the egg-eating snake of tropical Africa eats nothing else. It has a special adaptation for cracking the eggshell. It engulfs the egg, even if it is several times the size of its own head, and moves it down its gullet by contracting its muscles. The egg comes into contact with a group of sharp, bony spines, which are extensions of the snake's vertebrae. When the snake can feel that the egg is in place, it begins to wriggle about until the shell cracks.

Two things happen next. The contents of the egg slip into the snake's stomach, and the shell is compacted – rather like an old car body that has been through a metal crusher – and ejected through the snake's mouth in a neat package.

This snake can afford to have a diet consisting solely of eggs because it lives in tropical Africa, where one or other species of bird breeds all the year round.

Left **Being legless is no hindrance to movement. Many species, such as this rat snake, can climb trees and slide along the thinnest of branches. This enables them to pluck baby birds from their nests.**

Right **The egg-eating snake can swallow the seemingly impossible by un-hinging its jaws. The egg is cracked once inside the snake.**

Senses and Supersenses

The ways in which snakes find their prey are various, and in some cases distinctly eerie.

All snakes can see but they do not rely on sight, as we do, for perceiving the world. A snake uses its tongue to taste the air. In stories and paintings, the snake's forked tongue is synonymous with trickery. Even today, children are threatened with having their tongue split if they are caught lying. However, it is thought that a split tongue gives the snake a stereo sense of smell, similar to having two ears enables us to hear in stereo. Cells on the tips of the forks pick up molecules from the air. When the tongue is withdrawn into the mouth the tips rest near a sensory organ that detects chemicals in the molecules. Our sense of smell is limited, but we can pick up the odour of things like a wet dog or a heavily scented person. Snakes can taste things in much the same way as we smell them only their senses are much more sensitive than ours.

Many snakes stick out their tongue to detect prey, to find traditional hibernating dens, which presumably taste strongly of snake, and to locate a mate. Males can pick up special chemicals released by females up to 1.6km (1 mile) away. This is important because the sexes do not meet very often. A male can tell from a female's odour whether she is ready to mate and therefore worth tracking down.

When it brings its tongue back into its mouth, each tip is popped into a

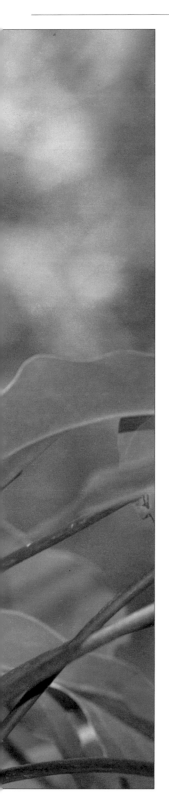

Left **Most snakes do not attack wantonly. They try to avoid encounters with large animals, including humans, that could harm them. When threatened, the Indian cobra inflates its hood to make itself look larger, as a defensive reaction.**

Right **A snake's forked tongue may give it a 'stereo' sense of taste.**

small pit at the front of its upper jaw. These pits are called Jacobson's organ, after the man who discovered them. They are liberally supplied with nerve endings that analyse the incoming chemicals and send messages to the snake's brain with information about its surroundings.

All snakes are deaf, in the sense that they have no ears. The traditional image of the snake charmer, hypnotising a deadly cobra with the magic of music, is a myth. The snake is responding to the movement of the snake charmer's flute, following it with its eyes, or to the vibration of his foot, tapping on the ground, and the shape and decoration of the flute.

If it is the vibration that charms the snake, it may be said not to be completely deaf, because hearing at its most basic is the detection of vibrations,

Above **Although snakes are marvels of adaptation, they're still vulnerable. The rattlesnake shakes the rattle at the end of its tail to warn other animals to stay away.**

Overleaf **The boomslang is deadly, but it's difficult for a snake with fangs near the back of its mouth to bite victims as large as humans.**

although usually in the air. The ability to 'hear' or feel vibrations in the ground is vital to many snakes as a means of detecting the approach of a large animal, which may indicate danger. When they sense a large animal approaching, rattlesnakes vibrate their rattles, to warn it to keep away.

The strangest sense that snakes use is very hard for humans to understand. Rattlesnakes share with pit vipers the ability to detect infra-red radiation, or very subtle differences in temperature between an object and its surroundings. A crudely similar human invention is the thermal imager, an instrument used, for example, to find people in collapsed buildings by detecting the heat their bodies give off. The snake's system is many times more sensitive, giving it a picture of its world – a sort of 'heat image' that we find very hard to imagine.

The pits that give the pit vipers their name are two deep holes on either side of the head, between the eyes and the nostrils. Some pythons have pit organs, too. At the base of each pit is a mass of heat-sensitive nerve endings, capable of detecting differences of fractions of a degree. They can sense the body heat of a mouse from several metres or yards away, in total darkness, enabling the snake to follow it even when the mouse flees down its hole. The difference in radiation is what counts, not the absolute warmth coming from the body of the prey. No matter how well insulated an animal is, there are always some parts of its body that radiate more heat than others, and that is all the pit viper needs in order to find it.

Having located its prey, using its forked tongue in the final stages of the approach, the snake strikes. It needs to use a quick-acting poison, so that the mouse does not run too far before dying: but even as its victim tries to escape, the snake can still detect the subtle warmth of its body, and follow the trail with its sensitive tongue.

Poison Fangs

The venom of snakes is another aspect that makes them repellent and frightening to most humans. People tend to think that all snakes are venomous, but the truth is that out of more than 2,000 species of snake in the world, only 300 can produce venom. Those that do, however, can be very venomous indeed.

There are two types of venom: haemotoxins and neurotoxins. The former, produced largely by vipers and rattlesnakes, break down the blood vessels of the snake's prey, while the latter, produced mainly by mambas, cobras and their relations, act on the nervous system, causing paralysis and death. Both types of venom are introduced into the victim by means of fangs, hollow or grooved teeth that make a hole into which the poison can flow or be injected. Venom is modified saliva, so as well as immobilising or killing the prey it begins to digest it from the inside, even before the snake has swallowed it.

Back-fanged snakes, as their name suggests, have their fangs at the back of the mouth, with short gripping teeth at the front. They are seldom dangerous to humans, having mouths that are too small to get a grip on anything much bigger than a finger. Many of them have very potent venom. The boomslang, or South African tree snake, is a good example: once bitten, its prey drops in its tracks.

Among the best-known front-fanged snakes are the cobras, whose fangs are fixed, and vipers and rattlesnakes, which have an added sophistication. Their fangs fold away when they are not in use, along the line of the upper teeth. When one of these snakes strikes, its fangs hinge down and forward, in a lightning movement co-ordinated with the opening of the snake's mouth. The advantage of this is that the snake can have much longer fangs than its skull would normally have room for, and still be able to close its mouth. The longest fangs of any snake are those of the Gaboon viper, which can measure nearly 4.5cm (1³/₄ in).

A highly specialised front-fanged snake is the spitting cobra, which delivers nerve poison through hollow teeth, each with a small hole at the front. Deadly as this may sound, it is a defensive weapon, not a means of killing prey. The cobra does that by biting in the normal way. When it is threatened or alarmed, the cobra rears up and squeezes its venom sacs so that the toxin squirts out as if from a water pistol, hitting an intruder that can be as far as 4m (13ft) away. The spitting cobra always aims for the eyes. The venom causes intense burning and is a most effective way of disarming any potential enemy.

The snake can react very quickly, and it is very accurate. Drivers in some parts of East Africa where spitting cobras are common keep their windows closed when they are driving near bushes or long grass, in case they are attacked. Since the venom causes almost instant, if temporary, blindness, they are well advised in their caution.

How Deadly Are They?

The potency of snake venom is often exaggerated, but some species are particularly deadly.

The most venomous of all is a sea snake called *Hydrophis belcheri*, which lives in the Timor Sea, north of Australia. It was discovered only in 1946. It grows to about 1.5m (5ft) long, and its venom has been found to be at least a hundred times more toxic than that of any other snake. It would take about 0.005mg (five-thousandths of a milligram) to kill a typical

*Below **The adder is Britain's only venomous snake, but it is not particularly dangerous. More people in Britain die from bee stings than from adder bites .***

70kg (11 stone) man. The snake is not dangerous to humans, even though there is no known antidote to its neurotoxin. It is very docile and rarely attacks. It has a narrow mouth and short fangs, which makes it difficult for the snake to bite anything thicker than a digit. Its mouth and fangs are part of its adaptation to hunting the small eels on which it feeds. This may be the reason for its venom being so poisonous: having only a small head, it has small poison sacs, so what little it can produce needs to be very strong. The poison is said to be very slow to act, so by the time the first symptoms of a bite appear, it is too late to save the victim.

Among land snakes, the most venomous is also from Australia, which, incidentally, has a higher proportion of toxic to non-toxic snakes than anywhere else in the world. It is the tiger snake, from southern Australia and

Below **Non-venomous pythons kill their prey using gentle but inexorable muscular contractions.**

Tasmania, which also grows to about 1.5m (5ft) long. Its neurotoxin causes vomiting and sweating, followed by paralysis and death within two or three hours. At one time, 40 per cent of people bitten by tiger snakes died, but today there is an effective antidote, and most victims survive.

To continue this deadly league table, which is no doubt doing serious harm to the public image of snakes, the *Guinness Book of Animal Facts and Feats* lists the following runners-up: the death adder (Australia), one-quarter as toxic as the tiger snake; the Asiatic cobra (India), one-twentieth as toxic; and Russell's viper (South-east Asia), one-hundredth as toxic.

Snakes kill about 40,000 people per year world-wide. Bites are more common in the tropics, where there are more agricultural workers and more slow-moving snakes, such as the puff adder, to get trodden on by chance. In Britain, which has only one venomous snake (the adder, or viper), more people die every year from bee stings than from adder bites. In fact, nobody has died from an adder's bite in the last ten years.

Stranglers

The majority of the world's snakes are non-venomous, such as pythons and boas, which kill their prey by suffocation, and the grass snake, which swallows its prey alive. Contrary to popular belief, the constrictor does not crush or mangle its prey: that would be a waste of energy. All it has to do is to be gentle, but very strong. Having grabbed its victim, it throws a few muscular coils round it, and takes up the pressure. Every time the victim breathes out, it tightens the coil, so that the prey cannot breathe in again. No bones are broken, and the prey quickly loses consciousness, ready to be swallowed head first.

Like other snakes, a constrictor has a jaw that it can disarticulate at will, so engulfing its prey is no problem. Having fed, it retreats to a quiet place, often up a tree or down a burrow, to digest its meal, a process that can take a matter of days or even weeks.

It is generally accepted that the world's longest snakes are reticulated pythons. They regularly grow to over 6m (20ft) in length. The longest on record, killed in Malaya, was exactly 10m (33ft) long. The world's heaviest snake is the anaconda, but there are some tall stories about anacondas.

GABY: TALL STORIES OF BIG SNAKES

I had a 3m (10ft) boa constrictor draped round my neck. It felt smooth and cool but most of all heavy. After ten minutes my neck and back were killing me. I thought it was enormous, but compared with the largest of its kind, it was a titch.

The boa belonged to Jeff Gee who breeds snakes for a living. What he calls his home I would describe more as a snake house. There were tanks and cages and incubators from floor to ceiling, all full of snakes. Sitting on his lawn with what I considered an unbelievably big but brilliantly behaved snake coiled in my lap, Jeff entertained me with some big snake stories.

In 1907, a Colonel Fawcett claimed to have shot a 19m-(62ft)-long anaconda in the Brazilian Amazon. That's certainly a whopper. Not long after Fawcett's report, an anaconda measuring 17m (56ft) was shot in the Peruvian Amazon, and an 18m (60ft) specimen was seen in the wilds of Brazil.

Is there any truth in these giant anaconda tales? Apparently there are several reliable reports of these snakes growing to over 9m (30ft). The record is 11.25m (37ft), but the Amazon is still largely unexplored, so who knows what is lurking out there...

Scientists have worked out (in the way that only scientists can) that a snake over 15.25m (50ft) long would be unable to move on land (they also state that it is mathematically impossible for a bumblebee to fly), but large anacondas spend most of their time in rivers, so use the water to support their weight.

In 1944, Emmett Dunn, a herpetologist from Harvard University, went on an expedition up the Orinoco in Colombia. One of his group shot an anaconda which they hauled out of the river and measured. It was 11.43m (37ft 6in) long. The party stopped for a rest and lunch. When they returned to photograph the snake it had gone. Presumably it had been wounded, not killed, and had managed to return to the river. Emmett was mortified.

In 1910, Theodore Roosevelt, former US President and keen natural historian, offered $1000 for any snake measuring over 9m (30ft). The New York Zoological Society has increased the value of the reward many times. It is now $50,000 and still up for grabs.

Left Having a large, albino Burmese python round my neck was an enlightening experience. The snake was surprisingly heavy but amazingly calm and gentle to handle.

Right Anacondas can grow to formidable sizes. A 9m (30ft) anaconda was recently seen squeezing the life out of a 5.5m (18ft) caiman in Brazil.

Love among the Serpents

The courtship and mating rituals of many snakes have a strange beauty, as well as a serious function.

Adders are often reported as dancing together before they mate, which is a nice idea but unfortunately quite inaccurate. The so-called 'dance' is a wrestling match between two males, to find out which of them is the stronger, and thus the dominant animal with the right to mate with a near-by female who takes no part in the contest. The two males rear up and twine the upper parts of their bodies round each other, often springing apart with a violent jerk as they momentarily lose their grip. The snakes thrash and tangle in the grass, until eventually one of them gives in to the superior strength of the other, and leaves him with the female.

Snakes' eggs have softer and more leathery shells than birds' eggs, but the shell serves the same purpose. It protects the embryo inside during its development. One difference between snakes' eggs and those of birds is that the embryo is sometimes already partly grown inside a snake's egg when it is laid. Another difference is that the majority of adult snakes do not incubate their eggs, though sometimes they give them a start in life by laying them in a mound of rotting vegetation, where they will be kept warm by natural fermentation for the six weeks until they hatch. Some pythons incubate their eggs by wrapping their coils round them and vibrating their muscles to create warmth, but desert the young when they have hatched.

Left **The colour of a snake depends on where it lives. Tree snakes are often green (for example, this Green Python in New Guinea), while those which hide in leaf litter are mottled and brown.**

Right **A grass snake hatches. The time it takes for the eggs to hatch depends on temperature. In cold climates, the embryos grow very slowly and sometimes it can take a year before the baby emerges.**

Rattlesnakes and adders are among those snakes that produce live young instead of laying eggs. The embryo is held inside the mother's body, enclosed in a thin membrane, from which it breaks free just before it is born. As soon as all the babies are clear of her body, the mother moves away, leaving them to fend for themselves. This they are well able to do, being equipped with poison glands, and the fangs to deliver their product, from the moment they are born.

Surviving the Winter

Snakes are usually referred to as cold-blooded. This is something of a misnomer, because in sunny weather they can become quite warm to the touch. What the phrase really means is that they have no internal control over their body temperature. Instead, they have to adapt their behaviour

GABY: FEELING RATTLED

Filming a rattler in the desert was much more disturbing than the snake-pit experience. I had to get much closer to the snake than I really wanted to, in order to get us both in shot. The snake was fiercely rattling a warning. Even though I was with snake expert Barney Tomberlin, the sound instinctively made me want to retreat: well, run actually.

Later, Barney showed how to extract venom. It is dangerous and no one but an expert should attempt to handle these snakes – in fact, any wild snake. Despite Barney's expertise, the atmosphere in the lab was tense and I was glad when it was all over.

The next day, an albino Burmese python hatched in my hands in front of the camera. This time, I was thrilled.

*Above **Milking rattlesnakes for their venom enables pharmaceutical companies to make anti-venom. A snake provides about 5ml (1 tsp) of venom each time it is milked.***

to maintain a suitable temperature. This often involves basking in the sun after a cool night, or crawling into the shade on a very hot day, as most other reptiles do. When snakes are cold, they can become torpid, slow to take avoiding action, and thus easier for their enemies to catch, and more dangerous to the casual passer-by, from whom they would normally flee at the first thumping footstep.

When winter comes, snakes that live in temperate zones have to hibernate, finding a secluded spot sheltered from the worst of the weather, usually a burrow, where they can doze away until spring. Their metabolic rate slows, so they do not need to feed while they wait out the winter. Some species, such as rattlesnakes and garter snakes, hibernate in groups using a communal den, perhaps a site in a cave that has been used by generations of their ancestors. Famous spine-chilling photographs have been taken in these mass hibernation sites, showing hundreds of animals, tangled together in what looks like a lethal snake pit. In fact, since they are all asleep, there would probably be little danger to a human visitor in such a place; but not surprisingly, few volunteer to join the slumbering throng.

When warmer weather returns, the snakes begin to stir. As they creep out of their den, the first thing they do is to shed their old skin, revealing a fresh new one underneath.

Shedding the Skin

Snakes need to moult several times a year, either because their old skin is wearing out, or because they have grown too big for it. Unlike that of birds or mammals, a snake's skin does not grow with its owner. Like other reptiles, insects and crabs, it has to slough off the old skin before it can grow further.

The first sign that a snake is about to change its skin is that its eye turns opaque. The normally transparent covering over the eye is a modified scale, part of the skin, and as soon as air comes between it and the eye the snake is effectively blind. This is no real hardship, since the snake has its sense of taste to guide it, as well as infra-red receptors if it is a pit viper; but snakes rarely feed at this time. Next, the skin splits at the upper lip, and begins to peel back, revealing a brand new, shiny head and bright

eyes. The old skin from the head lies loose, looking like a flying helmet, complete with goggles where the eye-scales were.

As the rest of the skin comes loose from the body, the snake crawls out of it, leaving it inside-out on the ground, looking a little like one leg of a discarded pair of tights.

When a rattlesnake moults, the last scale remains attached at the tip of the tail. As it dries, it adds to the collection of hard rings from previous seasons that make up the rattle. Warning other animals to keep away is only one of snakes' many defences against their many enemies.

Warning, Hiding and Impersonation

The ominous rattle of the rattlesnake is not really a threat, but a warning, and even a plea. The warning says: 'You nearly trod on me. I mean you no harm, but go away, or else.' The plea is more heartfelt and complex. It says: 'I really don't want to waste my precious venom on anything as big as you, when I could be using it to get food. Also, if I bite you, you might harm me. Why don't we just forget it?' The result is usually quite satisfactory to both parties: the intruder sees the snake, takes immediate fright, and departs, leaving the snake unharmed.

Snakes cannot display themselves too prominently because they have enemies that hunt them. Their markings are usually designed to camouflage and conceal them against their backgrounds. Adders in Europe mimic the dry bracken of the heathland where they live, and puff adders, their much more venomous African counterpart, wear the colours of the forest floor, the greys and dull browns of dead leaves. Puff adders are particularly dangerous to human passers-by, because they are so well camouflaged, slow to move out of the way, and highly venomous. Their venom is one of the most potent haemotoxins known.

Snakes are camouflaged for two reasons. One is to avoid being eaten, but the other is to conceal themselves from their prey. The best way to hide in a tree is to look like part of the tree. A green mamba, and other long, slender tree snakes, is able to hold its body motionless, sticking out from

Right A rattlesnake makes its warning noise with the collection of hollow scales at the end of its body.

72

a branch, as if it is a green twig with a bud on the end, lacking only leaves to make the illusion complete.

In North and South America, there is a large family of coral snakes, all of which are deadly venomous. They warn passers-by of the danger by advertising it with bright colours: red and yellow and black in bands along their body. (These warning colours are practically universal throughout the animal kingdom, not just among snakes.) However, there is another widespread family, the king snakes, that live alongside the coral snakes, in Arizona, for instance. King snakes are not venomous, but they display the same colours as coral snakes. The arrangement is subtly different, but it serves to protect the king snake from enemies, who confuse it with its more deadly neighbour.

Travellers in the North American deserts where these snakes live have devised a little rhyme, which is easy to remember and must have saved many a life. It goes:

Red to yellow, kill a fellow;
Red to black, venom lack.

The rhyme may not be great art, but it contains all the truth you need to know about these two snakes. If the red band and the yellow band are side by side, the wearer is a coral snake, and best left well alone. If red and black are next to each other, it's a king snake, and harmless.

King snakes hunt other snakes, including rattlers, so it is to their advantage to be mistaken for a coral snake by their victims, because coral snakes hunt mammals and can be safely ignored by other snakes. In this game of bluff and subterfuge, millions of years of evolution have produced layers of complexity that can be hard to unravel. For example, why don't other snakes avoid coral snakes, in case they might be king snakes? No one really knows.

The gopher snake also uses mimicry. It is completely harmless, but imitates a rattler, not with its tail but by hissing in just the right rasping way. This impressionist of the reptile world adds to the illusion of danger by vibrating its tail against dry vegetation, to make it the complete sheep in wolf's clothing.

Bright colours are usually a warning of danger. The coral snake (above) is deadly and should be avoided. The king snake's stripes are subtly different, (right) and it is harmless.

The Snake Eaters

All snakes are carnivorous, and they have the reputation of being the aggressors in all their contacts with other animals. However, even the venomous species have their share of enemies: resourceful hunters that can overcome the snakes' formidable defences.

The king cobra feeds exclusively on other snakes and also seems to be immune or resistant to their venom. The African file snake is a specialist snake eater. In fact, it is surprising that there are not more snake-eating snakes, considering that a long thin meal is just the right shape for a snake's digestive system: easy to swallow, with no awkward legs, it fits inside perfectly.

The monitor lizard is a large reptile that includes snakes in its diet and appears to have a high degree of resistance to snake venom. Mongooses, in Africa and India, are famous for their skill and courage in attacking snakes, but the most numerous of the snakes' enemies are the birds of prey, a few of which hunt almost nothing else.

Above **Several birds are specialist snake hunters. The European short-toed eagle swoops down on its prey. It must grab the snake's head immediately to avoid being bitten during the struggle.**

Right **Snakes have enemies, even among their own kind. Some snakes, such as the Australian black-headed python, specialise in eating other reptiles.**

The long-legged secretary bird stalks the African plains and kills snakes with its feet. It gets its name from the tuft of feathers on each side of its head which make it look like an old-fashioned clerk, with a bunch of quill pens stuck behind his ear. It struts about in the long grass, until it finds a snake, and then stamps on it. If the snake attacks, the bird deflects the strike with its feet and sometimes its wing feathers. It then repeatedly stamps on the snake with surprising force until it succeeds in knocking its victim senseless. Secretary birds are popular with farmers in Africa: they encourage them round the farm, to keep down the numbers of snakes, and rats, to which the birds are also partial.

Short-toed eagles are also well known for their preference for a snake diet. They attack from the air, seizing the snake in their talons so that they can attack its head with their powerful bill. Like a number of other snake-

Below A spitting cobra is a formidable victim for a monitor lizard to tackle but the lizard is not intimidated. Snakes bite when attacked but the monitor's scaly skin is either so tough the cobra can't pierce it with its fangs, or it has some immunity to snake venom.

Left **Secretary birds include large numbers of snakes in their diet. They kill the snakes by stamping on them with their surprisingly powerful feet.**

hunters, they are often said to be immune to the venom, but this is not so. Instead, they are well protected, partly by their skill and agility, and partly by their dense belly plumage and long legs armoured with thick, shiny scales which the snake cannot penetrate with its fangs.

Empire of the Snake

The flood plain of the Adelaide River near Darwin in Australia is ultimate snake country. There can be as many as thirty water pythons per square kilometre ($^4/_{10}$ sq mile). Nowhere else in the world is there such a high density of land predators; not even in Tanzania's Serengeti National Park, which has a wealth of prey and hunters.

Rats and adaptability are behind the super-abundance of pythons. In good years when there's plenty of rain, there can be plagues of dusky rats. The snakes feast on the rats, fatten up and breed. As there is so much food, nearly all the babies survive. Then, when the rats' population crashes, the snakes simply stop eating. A healthy adult can live for between six months and a year without eating; the snakes shut down all systems and wait for better times. They live off stored body fat and when this has all gone, they can digest their own muscles until they reach a point of no return, beyond which they cannot recover.

As there is precious little other than rats to eat, predators such as owls and dingos cannot survive on the flood plains in bad rat years. This means that the python holds the position of top predator.

Legends and Horrors

Humanity's everlasting fear of snakes has given rise to a crop of grisly tales and legends, featuring the snake as evil and supernatural, the enemy of humankind since time began. The authors of Genesis, explaining how the basic goodness of the human race was corrupted, blamed it on the snake that persuaded Eve to break the law and eat the apple. The Greeks told tales about Medusa, whose eyes could turn a man to stone with one glance. Her (literally) petrifying appearance was enhanced by the fact that her hair consisted of a tangle of writhing snakes.

In Madagascar, there is a tree snake with a straight section at the end of its tail covered in smooth scale. The local people believe that it drops off a branch tail first, to penetrate the head of anyone passing below. In Australia, there are stories about huge bush snakes that chase men on horseback, by putting their tails in their mouths and rolling along at incredible speed, like a wheel. There is no end to the false beliefs and tall tales that are used to express the universal fear and distrust of snakes all over the world.

The Bruising of the Head

The Bible predicts the greatest enemy of snakes. 'It shall bruise thy head,' said God to the serpent, speaking of the human race, and the head has been well and truly bruised throughout history. There is some justification for this enmity: where snakes and humans have to share the same territory, the large, venomous snakes can be a serious menace. Their attacks may be mostly in self-defence, but they constitute a continuous threat to workers in the fields or hunters in the bush. Unseen, unheard, they strike without warning and often with fatal results. The fact that the snakes themselves are terrified of people and would get away if they could does not lessen the threat, nor the hatred they inspire. In many parts

Left **The mongoose has a reputation as a fearless snake killer. People in India and Africa encourage them to live around their houses to hunt snakes, scorpions and spiders in the vicinity.**

of the world, they are killed on sight, venomous or not, for safety's sake.

However, some of the persecution of snakes goes beyond the limits of reasonable self-defence. The most notorious example takes place in the southern states of America, where every year they hold 'Rattlesnake Round-ups', in which thousands of rattlesnakes are collected and ceremonially killed. Sometimes the snakes are collected all the year round, to be held just for the annual event, which combines vengeance with cruelty in a way that is hard to believe. The snakes are beheaded and skinned, to provide meat – for those bold enough to try it – and souvenir hatbands to commemorate the event. It may be that the first of these round-ups was organised by the community while the area was first being settled, to put people's minds at rest about the horrors of their new home: but today, when the value of snakes as part of the ecosystem is so widely recognised, there is no excuse for such continued persecution.

The task of educating people to hate snakes less and respect them more will be an uphill battle. The enmity is too deep-rooted to be weeded out overnight. But unless there is a change in the human perception of these fascinating and often beautiful reptiles, many of them will become nothing more than a memory, fading like dragons into little more than myth.

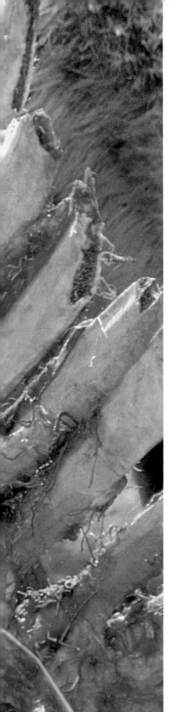

Chapter 3

Hunting Dogs and Hyaenas:

Predators in Packs

Predators that hunt in packs arouse a special kind of fear. A single enemy, it seems, is less of a threat than one that works as a team. A lone predator can at least be faced, but a pack is all around, attacking from all sides. Hunting dogs in Africa are now in dire straits, their numbers dwindling daily, but when they were abundant they were accused of mass attacks on humans. Yet cameraman Hugh Miles tells of lying on the ground in the middle of a pack without fear.

Hyaenas also hunt in packs but in the past they have inspired loathing more than fear. Historically, they have been seen as sly scavengers, thieves that pounce in the night. Their blood-curdling calls, the sound of manic laughter as they dismember their prey, have given them the reputation of the psychopaths of the animal world. Recent research shows them to be skilled and resourceful hunters, among the most efficient in Africa.

Left **Hyaenas are large – about the size of an Alsation – but need to work in a team to pull down large prey.**

Teamwork and the Hunt

Hunting dogs live in packs ranging in size from two animals to more than thirty. Each pack makes use of a home range that may be hundreds of square kilometres in extent, following the movements of the herds of herbivores that are its prey. The dogs hunt antelope, gazelle, zebra and wildebeest, that huge mobile larder of lean meat that fuels a great part of Africa's population of carnivorous animals.

A single dog, about the size of an Alsatian, is not big enough to bring down anything but the smallest gazelle, and anyway cannot run fast enough to catch it. The secret of the hunting dogs' success in killing is their group teamwork.

The dogs hunt in daylight, usually at dawn or dusk. They spend the middle of the day, while it is far too hot for the exertions of the hunt, socialising and resting, both important elements of their success as a team. They usually go to work when the sun is low.

A hunting dog has a cruising speed of about 40 km (25 miles) per hour, which it can maintain for hours on end. At the start of the hunt, the dogs lope across the plain in a pack until they come across a herd of suitable prey. Wildebeest are a popular choice, because they move in large groups and respond to the dogs' approach by stampeding, thus ensuring the success of the hunt. A herd that stood its ground would be safer from the dogs, but such steadfastness is not in the nature of the wildebeest.

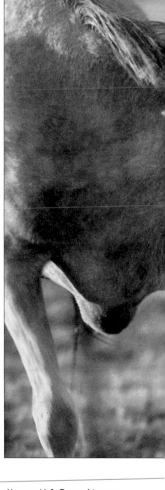

Above and left **By working as a pack, hunting dogs can kill animals as large as wildebeest. The dogs join forces to grab hold of their victim and pull it down: a feat that a single dog could not manage alone. While some members of the pack grab the wildebeest's back end, another will hold on to its nose.**

Left **Death is swift; hunting dogs tear their prey apart. This may sound gruesome but it is a much quicker method of killing compared with a lion's techniques of suffocating its prey.**

Above **Hunting dogs have quite distinctive markings, so the individuals within a pack are easy to indentify from each other.**

When the pack finds a herd, their first aim is to get close enough so that when they reveal themselves their sudden appearance will throw the wildebeest into a state of panic. They creep towards the herd, using whatever cover they can find. When they get close to their quarry they start running, with the inevitable result. Where cover is scarce, as it often is out on the open, heavily grazed plains, the dogs use a different technique, described by Hugh Miles:

'When they're trying to approach the prey over very open ground, where there's no cover, they crouch and get in line behind each other. They all creep along; they look unreal, just like rocks. When the animals stop grazing and look up, the dogs stop moving. You can almost see the wildebeest thinking "What's that?" and then going on with their grazing. The dogs get closer and closer, and then suddenly run. Then they just run them down.'

During the initial charge that triggers the stampede, the dogs are together, but as the chase proceeds they become strung out. When the leaders tire, they drop back and allow fresher team-mates to take up the hunt. Far from impeding the hunt, this tactic increases its efficiency, because the dogs at the rear can watch the movements of the wildebeest, and anticipate their turns, cutting corners to maintain the pressure on their prey. Early on in the hunt, the leading dogs select a likely victim, often a young animal, or one that shows by its movements that it is injured or sick. By harassing the herd, the dogs encourage its members to split up in panic, so that they can isolate the easiest victim to catch.

When the wheeling herd becomes sufficiently disorganised, the dogs move in to finish the job. Unlike a lion or leopard who suffocates large prey, hunting dogs and hyaenas tear their victims to pieces. It sounds gruesome but the prey dies usually in seconds, whereas it can take ten minutes for a lion to suffocate a zebra. The reaction of the rest of the herd of wildebeest is unexpected. As soon as the dogs have pulled down one of its members, the herd stops wheeling and stampeding, and stands placidly watching the dogs feed. They seem to know perfectly well when the hunting is over. Within minutes, there is nothing left of the wildebeest, and the dogs lope away. When they have pups they return to them, their bellies laden with food to feed their offspring.

Family Life

The leading members of a hunting-dog pack are known as the alpha male and female. They are a breeding pair, and usually the only members to produce offspring. They are supported by as many as half a dozen adult males. Although they have not fathered the pups, they help rear them. These males are born into the pack, so the work they do helps to ensure the survival of their brothers' offspring. In other words, they are helping to perpetuate genes very like their own into the next generation, which is the main purpose of animal life.

Females born into the pack can stay while they are puppies, but when they reach maturity they are usually expelled by the dominant female who may or may not be their mother. She will also drive off any other females who try to join her pack. Only when she is too old, sick or injured to win

Overleaf **The dogs start a hunt by walking into the middle of the herd of prey, in this case, zebra. They try to select a weak, injured or old animal that will be easy to catch.**

87

such encounters can another female, probably one of her daughters, oust her from the position of top dog.

The usual litter is ten, but the mother has enough milk for as many as sixteen puppies. When food is abundant, most of them will survive their puppyhood. Later in life, they will suffer from the attentions of their enemies, so only two or three will make it to adulthood.

Social Standing and Polite Behaviour

Because their survival depends on hunting as a team, hunting dogs have to maintain civil relations amongst themselves. In a typical pack, where high-ranking but non-alpha males frequently feel the urge and find the opportunity to court the alpha female, a code of polite behaviour is essential if the dogs are to avoid destructive conflicts. Each dog is acutely aware of his standing in relation to the others, especially the alpha male, and behaves accordingly.

The standard greeting is a soft twittering call, which sounds like an adult trying to imitate the whimper of a puppy. It may be just that, a deliberate assumption of lowly rank to disarm any aggression from another adult that might feel threatened by the encounter. As soon as the dogs are close enough together, rank takes over. The underdog cringes to his superior,

Above **Only the alpha female in the pack produces young. Although the average number in a litter is ten, in a good year, when food is plentiful, she can have as many as sixteen pups.**

Left **While their puppies are too small to join a hunt, all the adult members of the pack bring food in their stomachs back to den, and then regurgitate it for the youngsters.**

flattening himself against the ground, whining and offering his throat for any bite the boss might care to take. The senior male ignores this fawning in a lordly way, accepting his higher social rank as his right.

Relations with the alpha female are more complex. She is a fixture in her position for as long as she remains fit and strong, but the dogs around her can change their ranking from time to time. Because the pack needs a functioning leader at all times, another dog must take on the responsibility if the alpha male is injured or temporarily sick. When he recovers, his replacement may not want to relinquish his position. This can lead to some awkward social moments, when avoiding conflict becomes difficult.

For example, a complex social situation was observed in a pack of hunting dogs that was intensively studied in the Serengeti in Tanzania. The researchers gave the alpha female the name Kali, and her mate was a

seven-year-old dog that they called Homer. At the time of this observation, Homer had been displaced by another, younger dog known as Marcus. (No two hunting dogs have the same pattern on their coat, so they are easily distinguished; perhaps one day someone will do a study on how scientists think of the names for their subjects.)

Kali seemed content with her new partner, except when Marcus was out of sight, whereupon she responded enthusiastically to the advances of her old mate, Homer. When Marcus returned, an uneasy situation developed that was not without its comic side, though it contained a very real element of threat. Homer would cringe and whimper politely to Marcus, and then, as soon as his back was turned, pay court to Kali. Had Marcus not been a hunting dog, he would probably have torn Homer's throat out; but both dogs needed the other's support in the hunt. Instead, whenever he found the two together, Marcus placed himself firmly between Homer and Kali, elbowing the older dog out of the way. Eventually Homer got the message and allowed Marcus and Kali to walk off together without trying to follow.

Interactions like this puzzled the researchers until they realised the importance of courtesy and co-operation among dogs that have to work as a team if they are to survive.

Settling Down

When the alpha female is ready to produce a litter of puppies, the hunting dogs' nomadic existence must come temporarily to an end. The female chooses a site for her den, often the abandoned burrow of a hyaena or an aardvark. From then until the pups are three months old, it will be the base for the pack's activities. The alpha male inspects the den, but there is no suggestion that he has to approve of its location. More probably, he and the others are memorising its position so that they can find it later, returning from one of their far-flung hunting trips.

The puppies stay below ground, dependent on their mother's milk,

Left **Like all young dogs, hunting-dog puppies are very playful. During bouts of mock fighting, they establish a hierarchy that reduces the risk of serious fighting when they reach adulthood.**

Below **Hunting dogs, like wolves, have a complicated social system. They spend much time greeting and licking each other. This reinforces the bonds between the individual members as well as establishing and confirming their staus within the pack.**

until they are between three and four weeks old. During this time, the mother takes no part in hunting but relies on the males to bring food back to her. When the puppies come to the surface, still unsteady on their feet, she stays near them all the time: this is the most dangerous time of their lives, when they will need close protection from the whole pack.

The African plains are patrolled continuously, day and night, by hungry hunters, all of them potential enemies of helpless young animals. Among the chief enemies of young hunting dogs are lions and hyaenas.

Once the puppies are above ground, even when they are still based close to the den, they are vulnerable to wandering predators. Their mother, their father and their uncles must maintain constant vigilance if the puppies are to survive. Any approaching animal, but especially hyaenas and lions, will be attacked and driven away: the ferocity of the female at this time is spectacular and unmistakable. The rare accounts of hunting dogs attacking lone humans may refer to occasions when a wandering human hunter came across a den with puppies at this vulnerable stage.

After a visit from a potential predator, the female may decide that the security of her den has been compromised. Hyaenas in particular mark their territory with scent and droppings, and could well return at night in a pack to finish off her litter. She carries a puppy in her mouth to a new location nearby, probably one that she has scouted some time before for just such an emergency. True to the pack instinct, the other puppies will trot behind her as she carries their litter-mate, so that she does not have to transport the whole of her brood. Once they have settled in the new location, the pack will resume the daily task of feeding the ten or a dozen new mouths in their midst.

The prelude to hunting, after a night's sleep or a day's dozing, is a ritual arousing of the pack by the alpha male. He moves from dog to dog, sniffing and greeting, until the whole pack is on its feet in a frenzy of socialising. If their periods of rest give them strength and stamina for the hunt, this intensive social activity is what maintains the cohesion of the pack, stimulating the co-operation within the group that is essential for a successful expedition.

At the end of a hunt, the dogs demolish their prey until little remains, carrying food back to their dependants in their stomachs. The puppies greet the returning hunters by leaping at their mouths, yelping and licking until the adults regurgitate partly pre-digested meat for them to eat. Sometimes, if the puppies are insistent enough, the adults give up the entire contents of their stomachs, leaving nothing for themselves. While the puppies are growing, they are the focus of the pack's attention, to the exclusion of all else.

After about three months, the puppies are strong enough to travel with the pack as it resumes its wanderings around the extensive home range.

They are still not mature enough to join in the hunt, but they begin to follow the adults during the early stages, no doubt learning from observation and imitation the techniques of the chase. When things begin to get serious, the adults call the pups together and leave them lying still while the hunt continues without them.

This was the way of life of the hunting dogs all across the plains until about 1990, when their numbers began to decline so sharply that they are now among the most endangered animals of Africa.

Persecution and Disease

In the days of the great white hunters, when European tastes and morality were imposed across most of Africa, hunting dogs were regarded as vermin, and shot on sight, because their hunting behaviour was considered disgusting and inhumane. They were labelled as too ruthless to survive alongside the sportsmen from the north, who used high-powered rifles to fell elephants for their ivory and rhinos for their horns. An animal that tore large antelope limb from limb to feed its young was deemed unfit to share the plains with gentlemen who brought the same antelope down intact, before cutting off its head to hang on the walls of their homes in Europe and America.

It is difficult for us, today, to understand the attitudes of only fifty years ago, when oecology, then spelled with an *o*, was a word used by a few botanists to describe the new science of the relationships between plants in the wild. Advances in ecology since then have been so rapid that it is no longer considered revolutionary to suggest that predators such as hunting dogs maintain the health of the herds of herbivores by removing the sick and the weak. In fact, it is now known to be essential. Unfortunately, serious damage was done to the dog population before their role was recognised, and then disease took a hand to cut back their numbers still further.

Like all members of the dog family, and other carnivores, hunting dogs are susceptible to rabies, a lethal disease which has swept through Africa, carried mainly by domestic dogs. When the hunting dogs wander out of the open plains and into cultivated areas, they come into contact with farm dogs and those belonging to African herdsmen. If these dogs are diseased,

the virus spreads very quickly back into the packs, aided by their habit of frequent close contact during social rituals.

In 1990, cameraman Hugh Miles, who was filming a group of forty hunting dogs in the Maasai Mara in Kenya, watched them all die from rabies in the course of a few weeks. These were the dogs among whom he had lain with his camera, knowing them all by name, and trusting them as they sniffed him over and yelped their curiosity. Today, there are no hunting dogs in the Mara, and just a few survivors in the Serengeti, over the border in Tanzania. Another reason for their decline is predation by

Above If a mother suspects her birthing den has been found by lions or hyaenas, or that her youngsters are in any danger, she will move them, one by one, to a different site.

lions and hyaenas, both on the increase in Africa's national parks and other protected areas.

The numbers of these predators have risen because of the success of efforts to protect and encourage the herds of wildebeest. As the wildebeest population increased to nearly 1.5 million, their predators too enjoyed a time of plenty. Theoretically, hunting dogs should benefit just as much as lions and hyaenas. But while the dogs are true hunters who never steal from other predators, lions and hyaenas are opportunists. It is less effort for them to steal a kill from hunting dogs than to hunt themselves. As the dogs hunt in the open, their activities and successful hunts are easily spotted, and even a large pack is no match against a pride of lions or a clan of hyaenas. The blanket surveillance of the plains by hungry predators has meant increased pressure on the hunting dogs, especially during the vulnerable period while the pups are unable to move far from the den. Whole litters can be slaughtered, despite the valiant efforts of the adults to protect them.

Finally, the hunting dogs have succumbed to the pan-African problem of the expansion of the human population. Where once they had space to roam, even outside the borders of protected areas, they now find themselves trespassers on agricultural land. Farmers know that they are supreme predators, and even though hunting dogs rarely threaten domestic stock, it is easier to shoot them on sight than to risk the loss of an occasional calf, sheep or goat.

Howls of Laughter

If any animal was less popular than the hunting dog in Africa during the days of the white hunters, it was the hyaena. Universally regarded as cowardly, loathsome, filthy and a dozen other undesirable adjectives, it too was persecuted as vermin. Until recently, the best defence that could be raised for the hyaena was that, unpleasant though it might be, as a scavenger it had its rightful place in the ecosystem. Along with vultures and dung beetles, it was regarded as a necessary evil. Recent research has changed all that, revealing it as a resourceful hunter, with a complex and fascinating social life and a very mysterious relationship to other carnivores.

Below **Far from being lowly scavengers, it is often the hyaenas that do the hunting and then lose large parts of the kill to lions, vultures and jackals.**

Witches in the Night

Hyaenas occur all over Africa south of the Sahara, thriving especially on the open savannah grasslands that form the core of many of the great national parks. Over most of that enormous range, their reputation with humans has often been one of evil.

They have the habit of marking their territorial boundaries with

scented droppings, to warn off intruding hyaenas from rival clans. Unlike many animal scents, that of the hyaena is noticeable by humans, who find it pungent and unpleasant.

This ties in with a common African legend about witches and their nocturnal ramblings. Many tribes believe that witches roam the country at night, riding hyaenas and carrying oil lamps to light them on their way. When the witch reins in her steed, to examine her surroundings more carefully, she often spills her lamp, leaving a stinking patch of oil on the

ground. Finding such aromatic clues round the village boundaries was a sure sign that witches had been abroad, and that it was time to take protective action.

Given that hyaenas are widely supposed to be harbingers of death, and that a way to protect oneself against witchcraft is to rub pieces of hyaena flesh into small cuts in one's skin, it is not surprising that hyaenas were under attack from the Africans long before Europeans arrived on the scene.

Above **Circling high above the plains, vultures are quick to spot any carcass below them. Hyaenas watch and use these scavenging birds to guide them to possible sources of food.**

A Fierce Family

Hyaenas are neither dog nor cat, nor mongoose, but something loosely related to all three that has evolved mainly dog-like characteristics over many generations, and now lives a life more like that of the wolf. If that sounds confusing, it reflects the uncertainty with which scientists regard the animal, so much so that it is now placed in a family of its own, called the Hyaenidae.

The curious shape of a hyaena, its heavy forequarters and short back legs, is now thought to be an adaptation to its method of hunting. It pursues its prey steadily and relentlessly until the prey is worn out. Its jaws are among the most powerful in the animal kingdom, capable of biting through the thickest limb-bone. Its sharp, shearing teeth can cut away flesh in huge chunks. For many years, this was thought to be the equipment of a master scavenger; only recently has research shown that the hyaena is an accomplished hunter in its own right.

Above **Females give birth to two or three cubs in communal den sites. The young are born covered with fur and with their eyes open. Their dark coats probably help camouflage them in the gloomy light of their underground burrows.**

Overleaf **Female hyaenas use traditional denning sites to bear and rear their young. The burrows are usually dug by other animals, for example aardvarks and warthogs. Elephants have an excellent sense of smell, (as well as long memories) and give these dens a wide berth.**

GABY: FASCINATING HYAENAS

I had always found hyaenas slightly eerie and a little frightening. This is probably because they are portrayed as evil creatures of the night with immensely powerful jaws. They certainly do not look endearing; in fact, they look at best weird and at worse menacing. So you can imagine my surprise when I realised that I had sat quietly for five hours, with hyaena expert Paula White, utterly spellbound by these creatures. Some of her enthusiasm had obviously rubbed off.

I cannot describe hyaenas as beautiful, but they are compelling. As their hindquarters are lower than their shoulders, they look furtive and slinky. The sound of one crunching bones is spine chilling and its 'laugh' is eerie. You try sleeping in a tent out in the African bush with a clan of hyaenas laughing somewhere nearby.

Then there is the hyaena's clitoris. It is very difficult to tell the sexes apart because the female's clitoris is not only as big as the male's penis, it is also erectile. Somehow – and only a hyaena could do this – they mate and give birth through the organ. Females even have a pseudo-scrotum. I do not think I have come across anything much stranger. The reason for this is that the females have taken on the dominant male role. Personally, I think they are overdoing it a bit.

Above I learned, while visiting a local village, that the Maasai people regard hyaenas with respect because they help to dispose of their dead. Bodies are put outside the village perimeter fence at night. By morning there will be no trace of the deceased.

I did know that hyaenas are not skulking, cowardly scavengers but fearsome hunters in their own right. We came across a clan early one morning that had just killed a wildebeest. The noise was incredible; so was the speed in which they devoured the carcass. In about ten to fifteen minutes there was nothing left but a stain in the grass.

Hyaenas are scavengers as well. They even dig up and eat corpses in graveyards. I discovered, from talking to a Maasai warrior, that far from being shocked by the habit, his tribe value hyaenas as undertakers. When anyone in the village dies, the body is left outside the perimeter fence at night for the hyaenas to dispose of. The spirits of their ancestors can live on inside the hyaenas.

In some places in Africa, there is a special 'hyaena man' whose sole job is to feed scraps to hyaenas. He is responsible for making sure the animals do not wander off to another village. If needs be, he can even sacrifice a goat or sheep for them. This is not as crazy as it may sound. Hyaenas are very efficient at clearing up edible rubbish. In hot countries, dead animals, offal, bones and discarded food rots quickly. Apart from smelling awful, it attracts flies and can become a health hazard, so the hyaenas serve a valuable purpose.

Hand-reared and tamed hyaenas apparently make interesting pets, although they cannot be trusted near anything edible. They were even kept in captivity in ancient Egypt nearly 4,000 years ago. Inscriptions on tombs say they were tamed and trained, but not what for. I think I'll stick with my King Charles spaniel!

Social Life on the Plains

The social life of the hyaena is dominated by the females, rather like that of the hunting dog; but there all resemblance ceases. Hyaenas have a unique social system that is still not fully understood.

A clan lives in and around a communal den, where several females bear and rear their young. There are always young of differing ages in the den, the offspring of different mothers, but each female suckles only her own cubs. Most births are twins, but when they are of the same sex usually only one of the cubs survives. The dominant cub constantly attacks its sibling, refusing to let it feed, until it dies of starvation or infection. If the twins are of different sexes, there is every chance that both will survive: rivalry in the hyaena clan is within the sexes rather than between them.

Above **There are three species of hyaena: the spotted, the striped and the brown. The spotted is the most aggressive, and squabbles over food are common.**

106

Female hyaenas are larger than the males, and it is the females that dominate the community. They defend their young not only against marauders such as lions and hyaenas from other clans, but also against the males of their own clan, who have good genetic reasons for wanting to do away with the offspring of other males in the group.

The domination of the females is complete. Males rarely approach close to the den, for fear of the fierce matriarchs who guard it. A young cub of a dominant female can make an adult male back off, for fear of the consequences if its mother sees him near her offspring. The whole of hyaena society seems to be a fine balance between competition and co-operation, and ruled by fear.

The clan may contain as many as eighty members, who know each other as individuals, each with a defined rank within the group. They co-operate to defend a territory of about 20 sq km (8 sq miles) around the den, patrolling and marking its borders to deter members of neighbouring clans, and if necessary joining forces to fight them off in battles, which may be protracted and bloody, sometimes ending in death.

The armament of a hyaena is a spectacular deterrent to fights within the clan. They are equipped with formidable teeth, which are backed up by incrediblly powerful jaws for crunching through the largest and toughest of bones. They have the ability to inflict hideous wounds on each other, but they rarely do. To avoid conflict, they use a complicated system of competition and co-operation. The dominant members, which are always female, respond to a wide range of submissive gestures from their subordinates.

Hyaenas are exceptional in that both males and females appear to have an erectile penis. Males have a true penis whereas females have an erectile clitoris which is strikingly similar to the male's genitalia. Both sexes present their erectile genitals during greeting ceremonies.

Above **Which sex is it? A female hyaena's clitoris is erectile, looks like and is as big as a male's penis. Females even have a pseudo-scrotum.**

As well as their body language, hyaenas have a range of about twenty different vocalisations – moans, cackles and howls – with which they communicate at night. Being largely nocturnal, they need to be able to keep in

contact at a distance by using sound. To humans, the most hair-raising sound of all is the mad laughter, punctuated by screams and yells, of a pack of hyaenas on a kill. It serves to attract from far away other members of the clan to the food. Echoing through the darkness of the African bush, it is without equal among the sounds of the primeval wilderness.

Thief Turned Hunter

The reputation of the hyaena as a mere scavenger has vanished, overcome by research that has revealed it as a co-operative and successful hunter. The whole purpose of defending the clan's territory is to maintain a big enough hunting ground to feed all its members.

Hyaenas are prowlers of the night. They can hunt any tme between dusk and dawn. They set off from the den area in a loose group, fanning out along a selected radius. They hunt neither as a pack nor as individuals: because they can easily make contact with each other when necessary, they function as a blanket search-party, each alert for signs of prey nearby as well as to calls from its colleagues in the bush.

Their prey includes buffalo, zebra and giraffe, but also smaller creatures, down to mice and rats. At larger kills, during a hunt, as soon as one hyaena has grabbed a victim, other nearby clan members rush in. The first two or three will have killed the prey, not in any systematic way, but, in the grisly words of hyaena researcher Paula White, by 'eating it until it dies'. Their howling and whooping will soon attract others from further afield.

Young hyaenas take their place at the communal feast as soon as they are big enough, but no concession is made to the weakness of their youth. There is no attempt to take food back to the den, as hunting dogs do, though sometimes a leg bone or a head is carried there, rather like a trophy. The young cubs play with it and nibble at it; but until they can snatch their share, they depend on their mother for milk.

Recent research has established that 80 per cent of the hyaena's diet is prey that is caught by the clan at night. Nevertheless, scavenging,

Left **By the time they are four months old, young hyaenas have lost most of their black coats and have developed adult markings.**

Below **Hyaenas have immensely strong jaws and powerful, razor-sharp teeth. They can crush any bone except particularly thick skulls. They include a high proportion of skin and bones in their diet, probably because few other animals can eat them.**

especially from lion kills, is an important part of that diet, and the source of fierce conflict between the two rival species.

Most predators are specialists, avoiding competition with others in the same area by choosing to hunt different prey, but lions and hyaenas compete directly for the same range of food. Because of the combined strength of a pride of lionesses at a kill, a small group of hyaenas rarely challenge them head on: instead, they linger round the fringes of a kill, waiting to steal what they can or for the lions to leave when they have eaten enough. The lions, for their part, seem almost dog-in-the-manger about leaving anything for the hyaenas. Bloated almost beyond the point where they can still walk, they will sit over the remains of their meal, refusing to let the

hyaenas near, and threatening or even attacking them if they come too close. When morning comes, and the temperature begins to rise the lions move away to find shade. The hyaenas will move in to clean up whatever is left, down to the last splinter of bone. This typical behaviour, observed by early naturalists, gave rise to the hyaena's reputation as a dedicated scavenger from the hunting success of more noble beasts.

We now know that a large group of hyaenas can intimidate a small pride of lions and vice versa. More often than not it is the lions that steal from the hyaenas. There are a few records of hyaenas killing lions, but lions have often been seen killing hyaenas. A series of events in Luangwa National Park, in Zambia, led to a confrontation of a different kind, between a massive and growing population of hyaenas, and the park's treasured leopards.

Above **Hyaenas are fiercely territorial. They can hunt only in their home range and it is important that competitors do not deplete their food resources. When members of neighbouring clans meet, they will often fight and sometimes kill each other.**

Overleaf **Unlike vultures, which are solely scavengers, hyaenas can kill efficiently as well as clearing up after other predators.**

Rivals on the Plains

The hyaenas of Luangwa have always been there but in unspectacular numbers, up until 1987, when an outbreak of anthrax killed 20 per cent of the hippopotamuses for which the park was also famous. Four thousand hippos died in the space of a few weeks. Hyaenas are opportunists, and this was the opportunity of the century: they gave up hunting and devoted themselves to scavenging the remains of the hippos, until the meat was all gone. The result was an unprecedentedly good year for their cubs, as abundant food meant that all the mothers had plenty of milk, and at the time of weaning, when they were about six months old, the cubs themselves had plenty to eat. Except for the pairs of same-sex twins, where one often kills its sibling, the cubs all survived.

The hyaena population took off like a rocket. They were everywhere in the park, and because of the co-operative element in their feeding behaviour they were all able to find plenty to eat by hunting and sharing the proceeds. Every night, an unbroken blanket of patrolling hyaenas covered the park, pulling down prey, but also watching the activity of all the other nocturnal predators. The principal sufferer was the leopard.

Because of its hunting behaviour (see Chapter 6), a leopard is especially vulnerable to disturbance after it has made a kill. If a mother leopard is challenged, she will not stand and fight. She cannot afford the risk of injury, which might prevent her from hunting for food for her cubs for several nights while she recovers. Far better to abandon her kill to the intruder, and go off to find another. This was what the leopards of Luangwa did, leaving the hyaenas to eat the antelope that should have been feeding the leopards' cubs.

This was not the end of the matter: leopards are resourceful predators, able to adapt their behaviour to changing circumstances. They began to take smaller prey, and to disembowel it on the ground, so that they had a better chance of whisking it to safety up a tree before the hyaenas could find the site of the kill. So far, it seems as if the leopard population has not suffered from the explosion in the hyaena population, but only because

Left **Lions and hyaenas hunt the same prey and regularly steal food from each other. Competition between the two predators has turned them into deadly enemies. Lions will kill hyaenas and vice versa, but neither often get the chance.**

HUNTING DOGS AND HYAENAS

they were able to change their behaviour to meet the challenge. Not only in Luangwa, but over most of Africa, the growth in the hyaena population has had a marked effect on all the other predators.

The Last of the Hunting Dogs?

There may be a combination of causes for the recent sudden decline in the population of hunting dogs. Direct competition from hyaenas is probably not the only reason: in his long observation of their behaviour, Hugh Miles often saw hyaenas stealing a kill from a pack of hunting dogs. The dogs would fight valiantly, and even try to send lions packing. Sometimes they succeeded but mostly they failed.

Today, the combination of human persecution, disease from domestic dogs and the burgeoning lion and hyaena populations resulting from the increase in the number of wildebeest, has proved too much for the hunting dogs, which held their own for centuries in Africa's natural ecosystem. In the present modified version, in which many animals can survive and even flourish, it is sad to think that there may be no place for this versatile and successful hunter.

Above **When a female gives birth to cubs of the same sex, the bigger one will often kill its sibling.**

Right **The hyaena has been successful enough to grow in numbers recently, at the expense of other species such as the hunting dog.**

116

4
Grizzly Bears:

The Supreme Predator

The largest land carnivore in the world has inspired such fear, especially among settlers from Europe, that it has been shot to the brink of extinction in most of America. Only in Alaska does it survive in any numbers. Even there it can still be hunted legally, outside national parks and other protected areas. Tales of attacks by bears on people, of the fearsome power and bloodthirstiness of this huge predator, have given it the reputation of a man-hunter. No one pretends that it is a cuddly teddy, but there are ways for people to share the bear's territory, if only their prejudices can be overcome.

*Left **The Alaskan peninsula or coastal grizzly bear is the world's largest land predator. The largest on record weighed 751 kg (1,656 lb): ten times the weight of an average man.***

The Name of the Bear

The grizzly bear suffers from an unfortunate and unintended pun. Its name reminds us of horror or terror, but that is the meaning of the word 'grisly'. This bear was named by trappers who wanted to distinguish it from the black bear. Grizzlies can be any colour from golden blond to nearly black themselves, but the one thing they have in common is that as they grow to maturity their fur takes on a greyish tinge at the tips. It becomes grizzled (from the French word *gris,* meaning grey), hence their somewhat misleading name.

When it came to naming the grizzly for science, in 1815, a zoologist in a museum, who had never actually seen one alive, compounded the insult to the species. He gazed at its immense size and its huge teeth, and the whole thing made his hair stand on end. Being something of a Latin scholar, he knew the Latin word for 'makes one's hair stand on end'. It is *horribilis.* And so the grizzly bear became *Ursus horribilis,* now correctly called *Ursus arctos horribilis,* the hair-raising bear, wrongly translated as the 'the horrible bear'.

Unfortunately, a series of encounters between bears and European trappers and explorers did not help the situation. Being unaccustomed to meeting anything quite so large in the woods, they were extremely frightened of the grizzly. The grizzly, at first, was not so frightened of them: it treated them as it would any other unauthorised intruder into its territory, and warned them off. When they failed to respond to its signals, it attacked, and often killed them. They retaliated in the only way they knew how, by taking bigger rifles into the woods, and making a hero out of anyone who could show that he had killed a bear. Huge mounted skins were set up in hotels and gentlemen's clubs, standing tall and snarling, with the name of the hunter engraved on a brass plate at their feet. This was the heyday of Victorian trophy hunting: the grizzly bear was the equivalent of the African lion, or the Indian tiger, as the supreme trophy of the intrepid sportsman.

In airports in Alaska and the north-western states today, similar bears loom over the passengers in arrivals lounges to welcome them to town. And in most of the towns, the old nineteenth-century attitude to large bears persists. From all over America bold hunters come, clutching their official licences to shoot a grizzly.

Right **At maturity, a grizzly's coat takes on a greyish tinge, becoming grizzled; hence its name.**

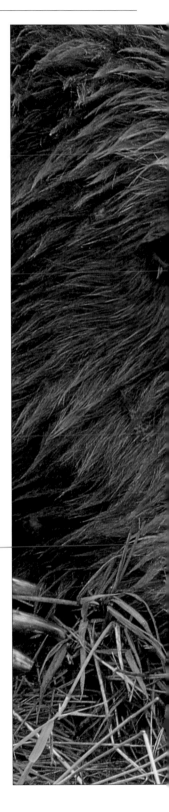

Killer Magazines

Their attitude is reinforced by a regular series of attacks by bears from time to time in which people die or are maimed. On every news-stand, all up the west coast and into Alaska, there are magazines for sale called, for example, *Bear Attack*. All the stories in these magazines are true, and every one is related in loving close-up – you could say grisly – detail. Sometimes it is a hiker or a camper somewhere out in Alaska, sometimes a visitor to a national park in Montana or Canada, and sometimes, but very rarely, a person going about his or her daily business in some mining town far away from the city. Some of the stories are new, but many of them are old memories, dredged up for the entertainment of the readers, who can't get enough of them.

The motive for reading these stories is simple enough: they give an urban American a delicious *frisson* to feel that right there, on his own continent, there are still fearsome things in the woods. It's true that a huge amount of north America is still wilderness, but the number of bears in that wilderness has become very small. The reason they are not increasing in number, and indeed still decreasing in most places, can be found in the pages of the magazines describing their ferocity towards humans.

In all of the 'lower forty-eight' states – that is the mainland United States excluding Alaska – there are no more than 1,000 surviving bears. Alaska, with its large national parks and vast unpopulated areas, has approximately 30,000 survivors.

Under Attack

The records of grizzly bear attacks go back to the earliest years of exploration in North America. A lot of it can be discounted as travellers' tales, exaggerated for excitement, and most of the early stories represent an attitude of hostility towards the wild which we no longer hold. But recent accounts can be taken more seriously, as indeed they come from the wildlife authorities in national parks. Each incident is closely studied to

Right **A grizzly's massive claws enable it to dig out ground squirrels, an important food source in spring when there is little else available.**

find out why the attack happened, and how it could be prevented from happening again.

A Mauling in Montana

The incident of September 1986, in Glacier National Park, Montana, is typical of many. Two hikers from New York, a man of twenty-six and a woman of twenty-three, were making their way across country to a remote mountain hostel. Both were seasoned outdoor people and had worked for summer seasons as assistant rangers elsewhere. They were at ease in the wilderness, but somewhat disturbed when they came across a place where bears had been digging, as they had not walked in grizzly country before. They knew what the books say about the proper action in case of attack: lie down and play dead, covering neck, face and head with your arms. They discussed it as they walked along.

Reaching their goal, they talked to the people at the hostel, and decided to go on another 7km (3½ miles) rather than turn back. Before they left, one of the rangers at the hostel took them to see a bear that was feeding nearby, telling them, as they watched, about his own occasional meetings with bears. He advised them that the best way to repel an attack was to yell loudly at the bear, whereupon it would go away. After a while, the hikers continued on their walk.

As they walked through a clearing in a wooded area, they heard a growl behind them. It was a full-grown grizzly, weighing about 200kg (440lb), as tall at the shoulder when on all fours as the man's waist. The woman climbed a tree, as the man stood his ground and shouted as the ranger had advised him. The bear paid no attention, but continued to charge, arriving at the bottom of the tree before the woman had reached the top. As it swiped at her boots with one forepaw, the man threw off his rucksack and began to pound with his fists on the bear's head.

After that, all hell broke loose. The bear turned and bit the man, dragging him away by the shoulder. The woman dropped from the tree and threw her rucksack at the bear, which turned and bit her. The man attacked the bear once more, to protect his friend, and took the brunt of the next round of biting and cuffing. He lay in the recommended position, trying

Left Alaskan grizzlies vary in colour from dark to light brown. Pale bears are often described as being 'blond'.

Above **Grizzlies normally do their best to avoid humans but some do occasionally attack people. However, unprovoked attacks are rare. Adult bears have short tempers and are easily irritated. A bear in pain is quick to anger and a female will defend her cubs if she feels they are threatened.**

to control his breathing so that the bear would think he was dead. After each of the people had been attacked once more, the bear left abruptly.

The couple lay still, aware that the bear was only about 10m (33ft) away in the bushes. They thought that it was watching them, waiting for a sign of life. Eventually, the bear began to choke: it had been eating the clothes out of the two rucksacks, and it seemed to have a piece of cloth caught in its throat. The sound moved further away, and finally the couple were able to go for help.

Both survived, thanks to a medical helicopter, and some delicate needle-

work during a month in hospital. The man had 66 wounds, which required over 1,000 stitches; the woman spent four long sessions in the operating theatre.

The local rangers and their supervisors in the parks service studied reports of the incident from every angle. They could find no reason why the bear should have attacked, but they were very reluctant to put the encounter down as unprovoked. As one of them said: 'Who can know what provokes a bear?' In similar incidents in the same area, bears had attacked campers who had food in their tents, which is against park regulations; a female bear had charged a photographer who had inadvertently come between her and her cubs; and a young woman had been dragged from her tent and killed: it turned out that she was menstruating at the time. All of these could be classed as 'provoked' attacks, unjust though it might seem.

In the case of the New York hikers, there was no such justification. One of the most experienced rangers, reading the man's account of the attack, was concerned that the bear had attacked from behind. 'That's what they do when they're hunting for food,' he remarked. No one will ever know exactly why some bears attack and most do not.

The postscript to the story is that the man, Jeff Brown, applied for a new job as soon as he had recovered from his adventure. He became a ranger in Denali National Park, Alaska. Throughout the summer, his job is to take people round the park, to show them the bears.

Spring Awakening

Spring comes late to Denali. The snow begins to retreat up the mountain slopes in April after a long, dark winter. As the temperature rises, mothers and cubs, and lone males too, crawl drowsily from the dens where they have been since October. They evidently enjoy their emergence into the light and air: rolling and stretching in the sunshine, playing in snow patches and on the brown turf yet to show the first touch of spring green.

The bears' first requirement is food. All the mothers and cubs can find at this time of year are roots and dried grass. Lone males sometimes may kill and eat small bear cubs. This could be due to extreme hunger or possibly to increase his chances of fathering cubs. If a male can kill a mother's cubs, she will quickly come into season and, if she remains in his territory, may mate with him. From the male's point of view, it is a good move, because it passes more of his genes on into the next generation.

However, the mothers take great care of their cubs during these first few days of emergence, especially if the cubs are new-born. They have already invested a great deal of time and energy in them, and they will not give up their investment without a fight. The best course is to keep well away from all other bears.

The cubs, usually two but sometimes three, are born in winter, in the den. They are already a few months old when they emerge, but they will be dependent on their mother for milk for many months yet. She needs sustenance to keep the milk flowing. Sometimes she can find over-wintered berries under the retreating snow, or a ground squirrel, which she digs out of its burrow with powerful paws. Ground squirrels are an important part of the bear's diet early in the season.

The cubs stay with their mother until they are more than two years old: they will spend two more winters denning with her after their first emergence. During that time, she will teach them the extent of her domain, the

Above **The Alaskan wilderness is the grizzly's last stronghold. Throughout most of the rest of the United States they have been virtually wiped out.**

Left **Bears are opportunists and will eat anything they can find. When they first emerge after a winter below ground, there is often little else to eat other than roots which they dig up with their powerful forepaws.**

right kind of foods to look for at the various seasons of the year, and how to behave in the presence of other bears. By May, though, Denali is changing. From its winter status as a deserted wilderness, it will become one of the most frequently visited national parks in the United States.

The People Are Coming

The travel season begins in Alaska in late May, when all the roads are passable and the weather has improved from the storms of early spring. People come from all over the world to visit Alaska's astonishing national and state parks, to see birds and salmon, scenery and plant life, but above all, to experience the grizzly bears. It is possible merely to sit in a bus and be driven round the park roads, and many people choose this option, their cameras whirring and clicking as they store the experience of a lifetime to take home to show their friends. Today, though, more and more of the visitors to Alaska want a closer contact with the wilderness. These are the hikers and campers who will take themselves deliberately into the realm of the grizzly bear.

For the park staff, this presents a dilemma. On the one hand, they want people to use the parks to the full, but on the other they do not want any more bear attacks, which would undermine the good work they have been doing to restore the bear's reputation. The course they have chosen in Alaska is to let people walk where they will, but to brief them carefully before they set out.

For campers, the cardinal rule is to keep all forms of food away from the camp. In organised sites, high platforms or steel strong-rooms are provided, where each camper must put all foodstuffs and any scented items such as soap or sun-cream. Any of these could bring a curious bear sniffing around, and set up just the kind of unexpected encounter that can lead to trouble. Away from formal sites, campers are instructed to hoist their

Right **It is thought that salmon are one of the main reasons the Alaskan or 'coastal' grizzlies grow so large. Every autumn they gorge themselves on the fish; an adult bear can eat thirty a day.**

Below **Bear cubs may look cute and cuddly but should not be approached. Their mother will be nearby, and if she feels they are in danger, she may attack.**

'bear-bait' high in a tree, at least 100m (110yd) away from their tent. Everyone who wants to walk off the paved roads must carry their food in a bear-resistant container, a strong fibreglass cylinder with a screw top that even some humans find hard to open.

For hikers, the principal rule is never to take a bear by surprise. Some people wear bells on their clothes, while others sing and clap their hands as they move, or talk loudly to each other. Others nervously chant 'Hey, bear' as they go. The principle of this is that bears in national parks know what people are, and are not afraid of them. If they can hear the people coming, the bears will move aside and let them be.

In Katmai National Park, among others, salmon fishing is the main attraction to visitors. The fishermen stand all day in the river, catching and releasing fish until they decide to stop, and take the one fish per day that they are allowed to remove from the water. Around them, the bears watch from the bushes, coming down to feed whenever they please. To avoid harm, the fishermen are especially carefully briefed.

It would be fatal if the bears were to learn that fishermen were a reliable source of free food. Thus the first rule of fishing in grizzly country is never to abandon your catch when moving away from a bear. On the other hand, moving away is essential if a bear wants to feed. The advice from the rangers is to move slowly, in a leisurely way: anyone who runs will almost inevitably be chased. The sight of middle-aged gentlemen wading gingerly through a swirling river, carrying rods with salmon on the end, looking over their shoulders and trying not to break into a trot, shows how seriously this advice is taken.

The Salmon Run

The salmon run takes place every summer. Millions of fish move in from the sea to force their way up to their breeding grounds high in the rivers of southern and western Alaska. Millions of other animals await their coming, among them 30,000 grizzly bears, and several thousand human

Right **At the height of the salmon run, the grizzlies catch so many fish they often just strip out the eggs from the females. Gulls and young, inexperienced bears move in to pick up the leftovers.**

fishermen. For the bears, a good salmon season is essential for their survival through the next winter. They need to build up their body weight by about a quarter of what it was when they emerged from the den, if they are to have enough fat to make it through to the next spring.

The bears congregate at traditional sites, often a shallow rapids or a low waterfall. They catch the fish by a variety of methods, some diving after them with a great splash, and others standing on the top of the falls, snatching the fish from the air as they leap up. The first-year cubs watch with great interest, accepting fish from their mother when she brings one to the bank. Those in their second or third year try the sport for themselves. The older bears, who have become experts, catch far more than they can eat, often merely stripping the roe from the ascending female salmon, and leaving the rest to the gulls and bald eagles that gather round the fishing ground, eager for leftovers.

The fishing places are crowded with bears. Females with young of all

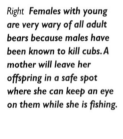

Right **Females with young are very wary of all adult bears because males have been known to kill cubs. A mother will leave her offspring in a safe spot where she can keep an eye on them while she is fishing.**

GABY: BEAR ENCOUNTERS

I wanted to see bears, and I was prepared to fly to remotest Alaska in a float plane to do so. I thought that was brave enough as I am terrified of small planes, but the flight passed through a thunderstorm. When we finally arrived at our destination, I was told we would try to film me a few feet from a bear. I felt no fear, only relief to be on dry land again. However, if I had known I was going to have a really close encounter with a full-grown wild grizzly (see page 142), I am not sure I would have been quite so relaxed about it.

I saw my first bear at Brooks Falls in Katmai National Park, Alaska. As soon as the salmon start to run up river to spawn the bears arrive from all around. There is a well-trodden trail to the viewing platform built opposite the falls. On the morning we arrived to film, a huge adult male was sitting right bang in the middle of river at the top of the cascades. As the salmon made great leaps to clear the rapids, the bear snapped at them in an attempt to catch them in mid-air. Every so often he was successful and took his prize to the bank of the river to eat it.

The salmon do not give in easily and fight to the end. They are a favourite fish with sport fishermen because they are such a challenge. They weigh up to 7kg (15lb) and are strong enough to

shake a grizzly's head from side to side, and sometimes escape.

Danny McDonough, our guide, told me that the bear was one of the biggest males in the area. All the smaller bears had to wait for him to finish fishing before they could have a turn. Females with cubs keep well clear of large males because they sometime attack and kill youngsters. I was quite happy to be watching all the action from behind the strong barrier on the viewing platform.

The next bear to arrive was a male, nicknamed Diver by the park staff. He started fishing in the whirlpool at the bottom of the falls. The fish gather there before making a great rush and leaping at the cascade. Diver had apparently learned from his mother to plunge into the pool

Above **When we landed at Katmai National Park, Alaska, I was pleased to be back on the ground. I'm more afraid of flying in small planes than meeting bears.**

and grab the salmon circling round him. He was remarkably successful and I was surprised that none of the other bears had cottoned on to the technique.

Everyone who comes to Katmai is given a thorough briefing on how to behave in bear country. The most dangerous thing any visitor can do is to take a bear by surprise. In order not to do this, it is important to clap your hands and say 'Hey bear' every few minutes. It amused us to find that all the foreign visitors, whatever their language, dutifully repeated the same words. 'Hey bear' in a Japanese accent sounds totally different to the American version.

ages and lone males gather at this crucial time of year to take all they can. This is an important time for the cubs, as they learn how to respond to other bears, adults and young. Females are very wary of each other, often threatening or sparring with others when they come too close. Males are given a wide berth. Although there is an uneasy truce in the general quest for fish, things are never quite peaceful, and the mothers in particular maintain constant vigilance. When the salmon season is over, they will be able to take their cubs away into the wide open spaces, to look for the other foods of autumn. Time presses as the summer goes by, and the only secure bear is a fat bear.

Food for Bears

Grizzly bears have a very wide-ranging diet, from roots and berries to salmon and ground squirrels. They also take larger mammals, when they can catch them. Some are out of reach because they are too agile: dall sheep, for example, can out-run and out-dodge the fastest bear, even though a grizzly can charge at nearly 50km (30 miles) per hour. Adult moose are too large and quick to catch, but their calves often fall prey to bears. In some areas, the bears have learned to patrol the bushes where moose mothers leave their calves while they go off to feed. A mother bear can make short work of a pair of moose calves, and in some years a small number of skilled bears remove most of the season's young.

In the autumn, when the bears' need for food is at its greatest, one source of food is provided by the caribou rut. Caribou bulls fight throughout the rut, trying either to protect their females or to take over another bull's harem. The bears watch all the time, waiting for an old bull, wounded or just plain exhausted, to wander from the herd. A mother bear, with growing cubs to feed, is quite big and strong enough to pull down and kill a caribou, once she can catch it.

Left **Grizzlies normally avoid each other, but every summer they congregate around the falls of Alaska's McNeil River, about 140km (90 miles) north of Kodiak. Fights occur, but not very often: usually there is an uneasy truce.**

Overleaf **As soon as the salmon run starts, grizzlies from all over the park home in on the river. They seem to know, to the day, when the fish are coming.**

Grizzlies do not abandon a meal that they cannot finish in one sitting. They cover it loosely with branches while they sleep nearby, and return to feed again when they have regained their appetite. People moving about in bear country are strongly advised not to go near any carcass that they might find covered in such a way: a bear is very jealous of its kill, and the owner will certainly be close by, watching for any intrusion. In national parks, the rangers put up signs on the roads near a bear kill, to warn hikers to keep away.

Another characteristic of grizzlies is their curiosity. Unlike a lot of other animals, they are willing to experiment with new foods, and this habit can bring them into direct conflict with people. Not only campers' aromatic soap and supplies, but the contents of people's kitchens are of immense

interest to a patrolling bear. In the little mining settlement of Kantishna, inside the boundaries of Denali National Park, one of the miners had regular visits from two bears, probably a mother and her cub, which had learned to open his kitchen door and his refrigerator, and help themselves to the contents. What drove him to take defensive action wasn't so much the inconvenience of losing his supplies, though in a remote settlement that can be a considerable nuisance, but the danger of walking into his kitchen one day and finding a bear. Once a bear adopts a place as part of its territory, it becomes very possessive and drives off all intruders.

The miner decided to establish his own territory, keeping guard over his kitchen porch until the bears returned. When they did, he duly yelled at them, as prescribed by the rangers in the park. They were unmoved. He then fired a revolver over their heads, with as little effect. When he tried to fire again at the advancing bears, he found that the gun had jammed. Just as he was contemplating moving to another state and becoming a bank clerk, his neighbour arrived carrying a rifle, to find out what the shooting was about. Between them, they shot one of the bears dead and watched the other run away, never to return.

Above **The easiest place to catch salmon is at the top of cascades. Salmon running up river to spawn congregate in the pools below the falls before leaping to the top. The bears soon learn where to position themselves so that the fish practically jump into their mouths.**

Right **Grizzlies have to learn fishing techniques. Salmon weigh up to 7kg (15lb), are difficult to hold and fight when caught.**

GABY: BEAR ENCOUNTERS

Grizzlies do not attack people on sight but a female with cubs will defend them if she feels threatened. A sick or wounded bear has been known to attack, and mature males have short tempers. The bears at Katmai are used to humans and are amazingly tolerant. We watched an amateur photographer leave another platform and follow a young male, who had just caught a fish, down a path into high reeds. The photographer was so intent on getting 'that close-up', he failed to notice the bear retreat behind a bush. The man practically stumbled into the feeding bear. He could have been seriously injured but all he suffered was shock. At least he had the sense not to attempt to take a picture!

In another incident, a woman fell asleep in the sun on the landing beach. When she woke she found a bear snoozing right next to her. She lay there for nearly an hour, not daring to move until someone found and rescued her. The bear apparently slept right through the whole episode.

Not everyone is so lucky. We heard of a man who had been attacked by a grizzly in Yellowstone National Park and went to interview him. Dan Shultis is a big man, weighing about 82kg (180lb). He reckons that his size is the only thing that saved his life. He and his wife had been back-packing in the park and

were sleeping in a campsite, alone and out in the open. In the middle of the night, a large grizzly picked Dan up with ease and shook him. The bear's canines sliced through Dan's back, exposing one shoulder blade. He also has slash marks on his arms and chest to remind him of the attack. Dan did not fight back or struggle. He curled into a ball and tried to protect his head. The bear, for no apparent reason, suddenly ran off.

No one will ever know what triggered the attack, although there were reports that people had been harassing bears in the vicinity the previous day. It is enough of a reminder always to treat grizzlies with a great deal of respect and caution.

At Katmai, the fishermen need

Above **During their second season, bear cubs are still totally dependant on their mother for food and protection. They are not weaned until their third season, but even at that age they have difficulty catching fish.**

to be particularly vigilant. The national park must be one of the easiest places in the world to catch salmon. The fishermen are allowed to take one fish a day; any others they catch have to be returned to the river. There are no such restrictions on the bears and they have right of way over the fishermen at all times. As soon as a bear is seen, people are instructed to reel in their lines even if they risk losing a fish, return to the bank and wait for the bear to pass. Recently (the season of 1993), one bear learned to steal hooked fish. When he started doing it daily, the authorities stopped all fishing in the area. They did not want the other bears to learn that people mean an easy source of food.

By midday on our visit to Brooks Falls, we had got all the film we needed of fishing bears. Danny decided to lead us through the woods and down to the river's edge in the hope of seeing a female with cubs. It is quite a weird sensation walking through a forest knowing that at any moment you could bump into a bear. It did not help to know that if you run, a bear is likely to give chase, and that a grizzly could come out of the stalls and cover the first 30m (100ft) of a track faster than a race horse. I was not particularly worried as I did not really expect to see another bear.

All of a sudden, there was a female with two young cubs walking straight towards us. I was amazed at how silently such a large animal could move. We had not heard a sound and she was already quite close. Following instructions we backed off slowly into the woods, clapping loudly. After a couple of minutes, the female passed in front, giving us a wonderful, close-up look at her cubs. We waited for a couple more minutes to let her get well clear. Just as we were about to set off, the female came rushing back, making a chomping noise and salivating at the mouth. Females apparently make this noise when they are agitated and nervous.

When she again changed direction, we were beginning to feel a little vulnerable. I remember Danny saying: 'If she comes into the woods, just back off and let her pass.' Fortunately, she decided to escape along the water's edge.

After five minutes, we got the OK to move out. We turned right when we hit the trail along the river and were walking quite fast to get out of the tall grass. When Danny stopped dead, we all concertinaed into each other. Right in front of us, there was a large male asleep across the trail. Again we backed off slowly into the woods and made our way to another path to the left of our original position. I just couldn't believe it when a second large male ambled

into sight. These two males, one to the right and the other to the left, were obviously what had upset the female so much. We all held our breath as the bear passed 6m (20ft) in front of us. At this point we really did want to be out of the woods. I, for one, did not want to be around when the two males came face to face.

We were relieved when, without further bear encounters, we reached the main trail. Danny assured us that we were never really in any danger, but it was enough excitement for one day for all of us.

*Below **Danny McDonough, our guide, has worked with bears for many seasons and entertained us with some hilarious stories.***

Rogue Bears and Coke Cans

The park authorities, understandably enough, would rather that people did not take the law into their own hands in this way. They have a sequence of actions designed to deter rogue bears, starting with letting off fireworks, then firing blank cartridges at them, and progressing to the use of what is known in the trade as a 'Coke can'. This is a hollow aluminium cylinder, fired from a special shotgun with a very wide bore. It hurts the bear, but can do it no damage. A bear hit with one of these missiles usually takes off into the woods and gives the settlement a wide berth thereafter.

If deterrence fails, the next step is to dart the bear with anaesthetic and remove it physically to some distant area. All the grizzlies were removed from the public parts of Yellowstone Park by this method, not because of any offence on the part of the bears, but because the public would not leave them alone. Accidents were happening because people thought that the bears were tame.

Relocation of rogue bears is a last resort, undertaken very reluctantly by the authorities. It can be a death sentence, especially to a young bear, perhaps a male that has recently left his mother at about three years of age. He will have to find a living in an area that is almost certainly already occupied and defended by an adult male. Unless he is very circumspect, he will have a hard time of it, and in the first close encounter with the owner, he will very likely be killed.

The Coming of the Fall

As September fades into October, the weather in the bears' northern home is beginning to close in. Snow settles further down the slopes of the mountains, covering the food supply. The cold weather demands more energy from the bears just as their source of energy is dwindling. The time has come to take shelter for the winter.

Bears do not hibernate in the strict sense of the word. Their metabolism

Left At the falls, the largest males secure the best fishing spots and defend them if challenged. A stare is usually enough to frighten a less dominant bear, but if that does not work they will bare their teeth, snarl or make a chomping sound.

stays at a relatively high level, unlike that of, say, a hedgehog, which comes almost to a stop during the winter. Bears doze in their dens, sleeping and waking, until the weather outside warms up again. This is why they need such a large store of fat to survive. By the end of the winter, they will have lost between a quarter and a half of the weight they took into the den.

For their first two winters, the cubs will share their mother's den. By the third, she will be pregnant again, and each will have to find somewhere else to shelter. The female cub will usually stay inside her mother's territory, until she has cubs of her own, but the young male will wander off to find winter quarters, and his living, elsewhere.

Unlike a relocated bear, dropped by humans into a strange place that may be the middle of a female's territory, the departing male will be familiar with his surroundings, and with the edges at least of neighbouring territories. He will be able to pick his way through the more dangerous spots, reacting to encounters with the owners in the way that he learned while he was with his mother, until he finds a place where he can settle down.

Hunting, Poaching and Taxidermy

Even though the grizzly bear is protected throughout the lower forty-eight states, and in national parks in Alaska, it is legal quarry outside the parks. Hunters have to buy one of a limited number of permits, and hire a guide to make sure that they shoot only the one bear they have paid for. It is an expensive business, which may be the main reason why people still do it: for the status they gain from it. Otherwise, it is hard to think why anyone today should want to kill such a magnificent animal, let alone travel huge distances across the country, or even come from overseas for the privilege. The bear hunters who come from far away gain nothing but the excitement of the chase, and a rug for the floor, and perhaps the admiration of their friends.

There are other hunters, however, who hunt for other reasons. There is a market for genuine bear skins, and pendants and cufflinks made from bears' claws and teeth, which is not satisfied by the limited number of bears that can be shot legally. A few backwoodsmen find it worthwhile to take their rifles into the bush from time to time to supply this market. This

small-scale poaching has always gone on and is difficult to control. Now, however, a much bigger market has opened up with large sums of money involved, and bear hunting has become part of organised crime.

The money comes from the Far East, where bears' paws are an expensive delicacy in the finest restaurants, and bears' gall bladders are an important part of traditional medicine. The criminals are home-grown, though they may come from far outside Alaska. Poaching is an established industry in the southern states, such as Louisiana and Georgia, but it has become more difficult in recent years, for two reasons. The populations of fish and alligators, the two main types of quarry, have declined under pressure from the poachers, and the law-enforcement officers have had many successes in bringing the poachers to book. As a result, poachers have shifted their effort to Alaska, to reap the profits from the new and expanding illegal market.

From the poachers' point of view, it is a highly satisfactory situation. They don't even have to shoot the bears themselves. All over the United States, they advertise hunting trips in Alaska, and sportsmen from far and wide pay to join in. The people who buy the trips are innocent, assured that the whole thing is above board, and unless they are caught red-handed they will go home still thinking the same. As they wave goodbye to their departing clients, the organisers have not only acquired some highly valuable goods for sale, but also pocketed the profits from the hunting trip itself. As the bears outside protected areas have been largely shot out, the poachers now take their clients into the more remote parts of state and national parks. This illegal hunting, fuelled by foreign money, has become the greatest threat to the survival of the grizzly bear in Alaska.

There is one other threat to the successful conservation of the grizzly,

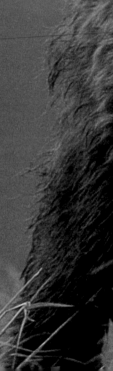

Above **One bear at Katmai National Park has been nicknamed Diver by the park staff because he plunges into pools to catch fish, a trick learned from his mother. None of the other bears have worked out or copied his method of hunting.**

Right **Many bear hunters have been so affected by seeing the grizzlies at Katmai, they have gone away swearing never to harm another bear.**

and that is the continuation of its reputation as a blood-soaked killer. The taxidermists are to blame. The people who mount the skins that are displayed at airports and in hotel lobbies are instructed to make them look as large and fearsome as possible. To this end, they invariably set the bear in a standing position, over 2m (6½ft) tall, with its paws raised and its mouth gaping to show off its teeth. They ignore the fact, though they know it very well, that the only time a bear stands up is to look around, and that it cannot, while it is alive, open its mouth that far. Bears fight, as they spend the rest of their life, on all fours. Unfortunately, a stuffed bear on all fours looks little more impressive to the layman than a very large dog.

Coupled with the magazines on sale at the news-stands, there may be more damage done to the cause of bear conservation in the airports of the north-western states than anywhere else in north America.

The Future for the Great Bear

There are still places where grizzlies are numerous and safe. In the remoter parts of Alaska and Canada, where people do not live and seldom visit, the bear is top predator, and under no pressure. Kodiak Island, in the south-west of Alaska, has the highest concentration of grizzly bears in the world, at about one per sq km ($^4/_{10}$ sq mile). There they were safe until very recently. The 4,000 native Aleut people who live on Kodiak have shared the island with them for centuries, treating them with respect, and valuing them as part of their spiritual heritage. Two-thirds of the island, more than 1,000,000 hectares (2,500,000 acres), was declared a National Bear Refuge in the 1940s by President Franklin Roosevelt, and since then the island has attracted a steady stream of visitors to see the bears.

Quite justifiably, the Aleut people want the chance to develop their economy. The best way to do it would be to build holiday facilities, such as hotels and cabins, and the airstrips to supply them. Hunting lodges would also be profitable: apart from the bears, Kodiak has large populations of moose and deer which could sustain limited, controlled exploitation. But all of these developments would put the bears at risk, not just from loss of territory, but because the increased human presence would inevitably increase the number of potentially dangerous encounters between bears and people, and the pressure for the bears to be shot.

In an additional twist to the tale, the organisations that would normally oppose the development are caught in a cleft stick: the other side of their responsibilities is to protect and encourage the development of the native peoples, including the Aleuts. The environmentalists cannot be seen to be fighting for the welfare of an endangered native species over the welfare of an endangered native culture.

The situation on Kodiak is an accurate reflection of the plight of the grizzly all over Alaska. Everywhere, the conflict is between the needs of the bears and the requirements of the expanding human population. As much as lions, tigers and any other great predator, the fate of the grizzly bear is in the hands of the people who want to invade its territory.

However, in the beautiful words of Earl Fleming, the American naturalist: 'It would be fitting, I think, if among the last man-made tracks on earth would be found the huge footprints of the great brown bear.'

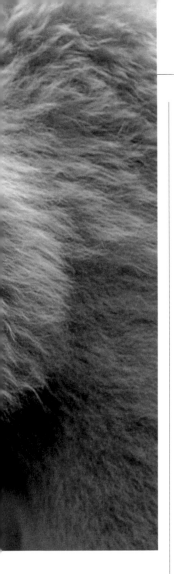

Above **Over the past twenty years, thousands of people have enjoyed the company of bears at Katmai. They have learned that fear of grizzlies is misplaced and that respect is more appropriate.**

151

5
Killer Whale

An Awesome Predator

Gliding into view from the dark depths like a sleek black torpedo, its streamlined form scarcely raising a ripple on the surface, a killer whale close up is an awesome creature. It can grow to 10m (33ft) long and weigh as much as 7 tonnes (tons). When it blows, a column of spray rises 6m (20ft) into the air with an explosive puff. The triangular dorsal fin of a fully grown male is 2m (6½ft) tall. After a vast gulp of air, the killer whale slides silently back into its element. With one beat of its powerful tail, it surges out of sight once again.

The killer whale is the most widely distributed predator in the world, being found in every ocean and at every latitude. It inspires awe and fear in equal amounts, and there is a deep mystery at the heart of its wandering life in the open sea. Many scientists believe that there may be more than one race of killer whale, perhaps even three. The behaviour of one race in particular may have given rise to the killer's terrifying reputation.

Left *The whales off the coast of British Columbia and Washington State were responsible for changing people's attitudes towards killers. When the first few were captured in the 1960s, they proved to be gentle, intelligent creatures in captivity.*

What's in a Name?

The killer whale was given its English name by the early whalers who spent their days hunting the open ocean for sperm and right whales, and watching in wonder the other sights around them. They had seen the powerful black-and-white packs tearing hunks of flesh from harpooned blue whales, and marvelled at their speed and strength. They brought back tales of this ferocious predator to tell round the firesides of British and American whaling ports. The reputation stuck. Killer whales have been feared ever since, until an accidental encounter in 1964 changed their image from psychopath to philosopher overnight. Since that time, people have tried to restore the killer's good name by giving it another: orca. Sadly, this is not much of an improvement. Orca was what the Romans called it, as well as being its scientific name. The Latin word means 'demon from Hell'. We might guess that Roman sailors were just as impressed by what they saw as the whalers a thousand years later.

A Change of Heart

The event that changed the human attitude to killer whales took place in Canada. A sculptor had arranged for a killer whale to be shot and brought to shore so that he could make a model of it for display outside the Vancouver Aquarium. The deed was duly done, but as the body was being towed ashore someone noticed that it was still alive. A hastily constructed enclosure was made from heavy netting, and the injured animal swam round and round, drawing crowds from afar. It was christened Moby Doll by the newspapers. (Later, it was found to be a male, but by then it was too late to change his name, and Moby Doll he remained.)

After fifty-five days recovering from his injuries, Moby Doll began to feed, taking 100kg (220lb) of fish laced with vitamin pills each day. Watching the whale, and encouraging it to feed, Dr Murray Newman, the director of the Vancouver Aquarium, noticed that it was making sounds that he could hear and record with an underwater microphone. In a historic broadcast, he played the tape to an interviewer, remarking that he was going to try to find out what the sounds meant when he had collected enough of them. It was to be another twenty years before the sounds on that tape revealed Moby Doll's true origins, though to this day no one has been able to understand their meaning.

By the time of his death a month later, Moby Doll had been visited by thousands of people and was recognised as a gentle, sometimes playful creature, nothing like the fearsome killer portrayed by the old seafarers. Nevertheless, the name of killer still struck terror into the hearts of those who met them in the open sea.

Reputation and Reincarnation

In a US Navy document published in 1964, giving advice to divers and others who might find themselves in the water on purpose or by accident, the authors stated with grim humour: 'The only treatment for being attacked by a Killer Whale is reincarnation.' They clearly thought that Moby Doll was a freak or a fraud. Earlier, in the 1950s, an area of sea off the coast of Iceland had been prepared for a navy diving exercise by being strafed with machine-gun fire from fighter planes, to kill the killers before they ate up all the sailors.

Below Resident killer whales are those which are seen regularly in a definite area, at least during the summer. They are fish eaters, live in large groups and are very vocal. Transient killers travel further afield in small groups because their prey, marine mammals, have acute hearing. For that reason, transients hunt without making noise.

Yachtsmen returning barely alive from shipwrecks in the open ocean often report that their vessel was rammed by a killer whale: although, as we shall see, this is about as likely as a boxer trying to knock his opponent down with his nose.

Yet the killer has another, older reputation. The Native Americans living along the north-west coasts of the continent – Inuits, Indians and Aleuts – have all known killer whales for thousands of years. Their attitude towards them could not be more different. They regard the killer as a friend, often a life-saver. They have many legends about how it came into existence, all of them stressing the gentleness of the animal, without disregarding its strength. They have every reason to know what they are talking about: in their kayaks they are much closer to the water and the animals that live in it than the chilled and awe-struck whalers, peering down from the decks of their ships.

GABY: KILLERS BY KAYAK

We had planned to take film of me in a kayak in amongst a pod of whales. A kayak was ready and strapped to the side of our boat. Strangely, I did not feel nervous about the idea, just excited. I had dreamed of going whale-watching, had talked about how marvellous it would be but never thought I would actually do it.

When we found some whales we became surrounded by about thirty of them. I am amazed we got any film at all. The whole crew was mesmerised and many of us were close to tears. There is something indescribable about killer whales. They have an aura and it touched something deep in our souls and emotions. We spent hours with the whales, although it seemed like minutes. In fact, we were so entranced that no one remembered to launch the kayak.

Above Encountering killer whales in a boat was so transfixing, we forgot to launch the kayak to get a closer look.

Birth of a Killer

Killer whales have a gestation period of fifteen months. At the moment of birth, the mother is not left on her own. At least one other female member of the pod, or family, will be in attendance, to act as midwife when the baby appears. Six births have been seen in captivity, the first in an American dolphinarium in 1985. As the tiny baby, only 2m (6½ft) long, emerged into the water, its mother's female companion nudged it towards the surface, urging it upwards until it could take its first breath.

This deep-rooted instinct has sometimes been shown towards people as well. Not only Inuit legends, but also a few accounts by Europeans who have been shipwrecked, relate how people in trouble in the water have been kept at the surface by killer whales, and brought safely to shore. Their habit of gathering round to investigate unusual events probably explains why killers are blamed for holing small vessels at sea. When a yacht runs into a half-submerged floating log – the most common cause of wrecks in the open seas – often the first thing the survivors see is the daunting dorsal fins and gleaming black-and-white bodies of a pod of killer whales.

Family Life

Killer whales are giant dolphins, and like dolphins they live in extended families, or pods, with five to fifty members. A typical pod might contain eight females, with seven calves of varying ages, together with two or three adult males, all of them sons of one or other of the females. Each pod roams an area of ocean that might be 500km (300 miles) from end to end. The families are matriarchal: that is, they are ruled through the female line. Both males and females stay in their maternal pod for life. To avoid inbreeding, the females need to mate with unrelated males from another pod. Where, and with whom they do this, no one knows.

The pod moves as a unit, its members synchronising their movements by calling. Sometimes they cruise purposefully along, and sometimes they seem to sleep, moving very slowly at the surface, uttering drowsy fluting sounds. At all times the water is filled with crisp, staccato clicks, as the whales investigate their surroundings by echo-location.

*Overleaf **No one really knows why killer whales breach. It may be to get rid of parasites from the skin, to communicate with other whales, or just as an expression of high spirits.***

Killer whales live in a world of sound, but sight is important too. They frequently stick their heads up out of the water, apparently to look around above the surface – a movement called 'spy-hopping'. No one knows just how well they see, either above or below the surface, but in murky water and the inky depths of the oceans, they are undoubtedly guided by sound. Apart from their vocalisations, they use their fins and tail to communicate, slapping the water to raise a thunderous splash, audible from far away. The ultimate splash signal is called 'breaching', in which the whale launches itself into the air, its whole body breaking the surface. Before it falls back, it often turns sideways, as if to maximise the impact.

Whale-watchers have suggested many reasons for breaching. Some say that it is a way of removing parasites from the skin; others propose that it is used in communication, or that it demonstrates the whale's strength and vigour, as part of a sexual display. On occasion, it could simply be an expression of exuberance. The glory of whale studies is that we do not understand what their actions mean to themselves or to other whales.

The Mystery of the Rubbing Beach

In one or two isolated places, the best known of which is in Robson Bight, at the northern end of Vancouver Island, killer whales gather to perform a ritual whose meaning is a complete mystery. Some drop in as they are passing, while others come from far away, making a bee-line for the small sheltered cove known to scientists as the Rubbing Beach.

When they arrive, they swim along the bottom of the shallow water, turning sideways to rub their flanks on the smooth pebbles. The movements look luxurious, almost erotic; and the whales utter calls that are never heard anywhere else. The Rubbing Beach is one of only a few places where wild killer whales have been seen to give birth, and on at least one occasion a young male was seen to be conspicuously aroused as his group enjoyed a prolonged session of rubbing, on the sea-bed and on each other.

Parents with young whales evidently enjoy physical contact. The youngsters climb on their mothers' backs and swim close alongside them, touching as much as possible. In the thick kelp beds of the shallow waters among the San Juan Islands, off the coast of Washington State, the resident killer

Above **No two killer whales have identical saddle patches and dorsal fins, so it is possible to distinguish inviduals from each other.**

whales often gather strands of seaweed on their dorsal fins, towing it along like a dog carrying a stick. They appear to do it for pleasure, and the smooth slippery feeling of kelp against skin probably feels good.

The killer's skin looks tough and leathery, but is in fact only about a millimetre or so thick, and very sensitive. The smoothly rounded pebbles of the Rubbing Beach seem to be of just the right size or texture to produce the perfect sensation. On the other hand, this place might be special to whales for some reason that is completely beyond our capacity to understand. Whatever the attraction, the whales' voices seem to indicate that they are glad to be there. Behind the whispered calls they make in this unique place, the faint click of echo-location is muted, as if the whales sense that here they are safe.

Overleaf **We are so strongly oriented to sight it is virtually impossible for us to imagine how killer whales find their way and hunt by sound underwater. They can emit more than 500 clicks per second, and many scientists believe they form a detailed 'sound map' of their surroundings.**

Echoes in the Dark

The echo-location system of killer whales is amazingly accurate. It has been shown that they can distinguish between a cod and a salmon at 60m (197ft) merely by listening to the echoes of the stream of clicks they produce in their nasal area. The front of the skull is concave, like the reflector of a car headlamp, to focus the sound. (The domed forehead that conceals this shape is filled with a fatty substance called spermaceti, part of the whale's adaptation to diving to great depths without damage.) As the echoes return through the water, the whale receives them at the point of its lower jaw, from where they are transmitted in oil-filled channels to its ears. This delicate receiving area, through which the killer obtains all its information about its surroundings, is supposed to be the part of its anatomy with which it rams and sinks yachts!

Most of the killer's massive brain is dedicated to interpreting the echoes it hears, giving it a very elaborate sound picture of its surroundings. When

Right Killer whales live in a world of sound, but sight is important too. They often raise themselves vertically out of the water, apparently to have a good look around.

Below Killer whales belong to the family of toothed whales. They have an impressive array of teeth for catching and grasping fish, or tearing apart marine mammals.

the whales are at ease, the sounds they produce are intermittent and soft. When they are hunting, they utter streams of louder and more rapid clicks, to obtain a more detailed image of their prey.

Occasionally, researchers listening with hydrophones have been astonished to hear single, very loud bangs from hunting whales, enough to make their ears ring. One suggestion is that these violent explosions are used by the whales to stun fish, to make them easier to catch.

Rivalry and Retribution

Killer whales that are seen regularly in a known area are known as 'residents'. These whales are very efficient hunters of fish, especially during the spring and summer salmon runs when the fish are moving from the ocean to the rivers where they breed. At one time, people thought that the whales always co-operated, hunting as a team to round up as many fish as possible. Watching a hunting party from the surface, and listening to their vocalisations on hydrophones, it is now known that they also work singly. It depends on the location and the number of fish.

A remarkable piece of recent film shows killer whales hunting herring using a completely different technique. Instead of hurling themselves into the shoal, the whales circled it, forcing the fish to form a tight ball near the surface. Others from the pod dived amongst the herring, stunning them with mighty blows from their tails. When the herring were immobilised, the whales moved in one by one to pick out individual fish to eat.

The difference in style is a reaction to the different behaviour of the fish being preyed upon. Salmon moving inshore to breed are a mass of individuals, each intent on its own pilgrimage to the spawning grounds. They are not gregarious in the same way as other fish that form shoals for mutual protection. The only reason for the huge numbers of salmon moving about together is the coincidence of the season: they all need to breed at the same time of year. Herring, on the other hand, are shoaling fish: under threat, they crowd into a dense pack to confuse predators and to increase

Left The killer whales's breeding strategy is a bit of a mystery. To avoid inbreeding, females must mate with unrelated males from outside their own pod. Resident pods often meet and mingle, and perhaps it is at these occasions that mating takes place.

each individual's chance of survival. The killer whales modify their hunting behaviour to take advantage of this, and reap a generous reward.

Such efficiency arouses envy among human fishermen. As the salmon season starts each year, the killer whales gather in the same area as the men with boats and nets. Some fishermen regard the whales as competition and occasionally resort to shooting at them in an effort to protect what they see as their fish stocks. In Prince William Sound, Alaska, long a prime salmon-fishing area, many of the killer whales bear the scars of rifle bullets, and not a few have died at the hands of envious fishermen. It is illegal to harm killer whales, but all the protective legislation in the world will not save the whales from attack in such a lonely, remote place. Fortunately, it is not easy to kill a killer with a rifle, and the fishermen are beginning to regard killer whales in a better light.

Below **Killers have their first calf at about fourteen, and then one every five or six years after until they reach their forties. Both male and female calves stay in their natal pods for life. This is thought to be a unique social system within the animal kingdom.**

The Language of the Killer

The calls of killer whales have been the subject of intense study since the first historic recording of them by Murray Newman in 1964. Although no one has found a way of interpreting the signals, they are certainly some form of code or language. Soft twittering sounds are mixed with swooping whistles and harsh grating noises, answered by nearby animals. They can be heard from a great distance; researchers often hear the whales coming before they can see them.

Even though they are impossible to understand, the calls have served a very useful purpose in whale studies. Each pod has its own distinct dialect, using about a dozen combinations of sounds not made by any other pod. A call started by one animal is usually taken up by the others, as if in agreement, or perhaps to reassure all within earshot that the family is intact. The dialects survive for many generations, being passed on by older pod members to the youngsters as they grow up, and taught by them in turn to new members.

One of the resident pods near Vancouver Island had been studied for twenty years before the scientist in charge, Mike Biggs, heard the old recording of Moby Doll. He recognised the dialect at once. In his lonely agony, trapped inside his makeshift prison, Moby Doll had been calling out to his family in the language that was theirs alone.

Photographic Evidence

The identity of the pods and their members has been worked out by long-term studies, using photographs of the dorsal fin and the grey 'saddle' at the base of the fin. The markings of each killer whale are different from all others, as distinct as one fingerprint from another. In this way, the structure of the pods has become clear, revealing that a senior female rules the roost, accompanied by her daughters, sons, nieces and nephews, and usually one, or sometimes two or more, large senior males. Killer whales can live for seventy or eighty years in the wild.

One unexpected result of these photographic studies was to confirm a theory advanced by Russian scientists working in the Antarctic, suggesting that there might be more than one race of killer whale.

Overleaf **Adult males have much taller dorsal fins than females. The average life span for males is about thirty years, compared with fifty for females, but there is evidence that they can live into their mid-eighties.**

Wandering Whales

After years of comparing fin shapes and the markings on the backs of whales, the North American researchers realised that some of the whales they had been photographing had fins that were distinctly different in their general shape from those of the pod members they saw every day. These whales appeared irregularly, at long intervals, moving in small pods. To distinguish them from the resident pods, they called the strangers 'transients'. As the scientists learned to recognise these infrequent visitors, they found that they were very different in their behaviour, as well as in their appearance.

For one thing, the transients evidently moved huge distances, being seen and recognised by watchers as far apart as western Alaska and California. For another, their voices were quite different, on the rare occasions when they could be heard. The third distinction was in their diet: transients hunt other marine mammals, mainly seals, sea-lions and porpoises. Off the Californian coast they hunt grey whales and around Antarctica, penguins are a favourite prey. This accounts for their usually silent movements: unlike fish, mammals have good hearing.

When one of the scientists came across the results of the Russian survey in a technical publication, things began to fall into place. The Russians had killed a couple of hundred killer whales over several years, as part of a study into their population structure and longevity. In the course of the work, they had carried out the usual measurements of skulls and teeth, filling pages of notebooks with columns of figures. Unlike the Americans, the Russians had not watched the behaviour of the whales before they killed them, so they had no explanation for the curious fact that the measurements fell into two quite distinct groups, as if there might be two separate subspecies of killer whale. These investigations, taken together with the American observations of the difference in behaviour, now seemed to show that this was the case.

Subsequently, studies of the DNA of the two groups have shown that the two subspecies have not interbred for a 100,000 years. Now yet another group has been discovered, called 'offshores' because they seldom come near land.

GABY: THE HARMLESS KILLERS

Many years ago, I was lucky enough to swim with dolphins. It was a moving experience that affected me deeply, but being with killer whales made me feel euphoric.

Trying to film me with the whales in the background, off the end of our boat, was a tall order. Killer whales don't travel in straight lines or at any given speed. Trying to guess where they would come up was harder than predicting the location of the football in a photographic goal quiz.

To this day, I am convinced that the whales knew we were filming them. We were all set up, everyone was ready and the whales suddenly appeared directly behind the boat, milling

Above **Howard Garrett of the Center for Whale Research on the San Juan islands took us whale-watching. He could recognise all the local resident killers and was a mine of information.**

Below **Whale-watching is now a very popular leisure activity. The whales seem not to mind boats as long as they keep a respectful distance away and avoid revving their engine.**

around. Two killers stuck their heads out of the water just behind me, then a big male swam right up to the boat, rolled on to his side and took a good long look at me. I was supposed to be saying something deep and meaningful to camera, but all I could do was stand there with tears running down my face and say 'Wow!'

Many people have said that being with whales is a healing experience. They certainly have a strange, almost spiritual aura. I can understand why the local native people believe that the spirits of their ancestors live on in these creatures.

People now come from all over the world to watch killer whales. For some, it is a once in a lifetime pilgrimage; for others it is an annual event. For me it is an experience I shall always carry in my heart.

GABY: THE PORPOISE PUZZLE

Killer whales had been sighted in Haro Strait. This was not far from Friday Harbor in the San Juan Islands, where we had come in the hope of seeing these whales. We scrambled on to our waiting boat and set out to sea.

Fifteen minutes later we came across not killers but a pair of Pacific white-sided dolphins behaving in a very strange way. On closer inspection, we could see that they were reacting to a very young, possibly new-born, harbour porpoise. They were not exactly playing with it, nor were they being aggressive. It appeared that they were trying to keep it afloat and active. Sometimes they even looked as if they were lifting it out of the water, so that it could breathe.

The baby porpoise's mother was nowhere to be seen but there were reports that a group of resident killer whales had just passed through the area. Our whale experts explained that since they were residents, it was possible but unlikely that they had killed the baby porpoise's mother. Residents have been seen to kill and eat marine mammals in the area but only rarely. On hearing the whales approach, the adult porpoises may have panicked and swum away too fast for the baby to keep up.

We will never know what really happened. What we do know is that the dolphins stayed with the young porpoise for the next four hours. They may have been trying to save it but they could not feed it. Eventually, it became weak and distressed. Later we heard that scientists from the Marine Mammal Research Group in Victoria captured the little porpoise and took it to the Point Defiance Zoo in Tacoma.

Removing the baby caused a certain amount of controversy. Some whale researchers argue that the porpoise was worth saving, since it was young enough to adapt well to captivity and could provide valuable information for future research. Many people feel that the more we learn about the whale family, even in captivity, the more we can help those in the wild. Others feel that nature should be allowed to take her course and that humans should not interfere. Many people think that any mammal designed to roam the open sea would be better off dead than confined to a small pool for life.

The baby harbour porpoise died four days later.

Below **Dolphins are really a type of small whale. Some species are solitary, while others are highly gregarious. Lone dolphins have been known to befriend swimmers and sailors.**

The Elusive Offshores

There is so much we do not know about the lives and habits of killer whales. We know almost nothing about their sexual behaviour, or the meaning behind their complicated calls. When the residents disappear out to sea, where to they go, what do they feed on, and do they join up with other whales?

No one knows the answer but one possibility is that they join up with a newly discovered group of orcas, called 'offshores'. These killer whales live in large groups of up to seventy individuals. They have a distinctive dialect which is very different to the dialects of all known resident and transient pods. As well, their dorsal fin is slightly different to the other types of killers.

Recent research has showed that offshores are fish eaters like resident orcas. A group of seventy whales would find it hard to hunt marine mammals, since they would have difficulty taking them by surprise. One large pod spent a winter off the coast of California feeding on huge shoals of herring. Members from the same pod have also been seen off the coast of Alaska and round Vancouver Island, so at least we now know that they can travel great distances.

Another group of nine offshores recently got themselves trapped in Barnes Lake on the Alaskan coast. The sea flows into the lake only on the highest tides. At low tide it becomes an inland water, cut off from the ocean. It is thought the whales swam into the lake on a high tide while they were chasing fish. The lake is about 16km long and 3 to 5km wide (10 x 2 to 3 miles). When the tide went out the whales seemed to sense that they were trapped. They became agitated and disorientated. Even when the next high tide gave them an escape route, they were unable to do anything more than swim around in panic.

When one killer was found dead, the authorities decided to herd the whales out to sea on the next high tide. Unfortunately, a second whale died in the interim period but the remaining seven made it. On returning to the open ocean, the whales appeared to relax and several of them breached repeatedly as if signalling their joy at finding freedom. If an orca's sonar system can inform it that it is trapped in a space this size, what must a captive killer whale in a pool feel like?

The Killers of Punta Norte

Some of the best places to see the power of killer whales in action are the beaches of Patagonia, in southern Argentina. One in particular, near Punta Norte, has been studied and photographed extensively, as the whales beach themselves to catch and kill seals and sea-lions at the water's edge.

The hunters are not transients, as one might expect, but a pod of resident whales. They have evidently learned that marine mammals are a nourishing alternative to fish, and that this beach has the right configuration to make them easy to catch.

The shape of the beach at low tide reveals its value to the whales. A deep gully cuts through the beach rock, where seals and sea-lions bask, before the steep slope leading to the low-water mark. As the tide rises, the gully is flooded, until the waves are lapping over the rock to a depth of a few feet. High-tide mark is among loose pebbles, warmed by the sun. Driven up the beach by the rising water, the seals and sea-lions roll and snooze among the pebbles, protected from attack from the sea by the ridge of beach rock; all except in one place, where the gully provides a channel of

Above **The killers of Punta Norte in Argentina have learned to patrol the beaches in search of unwary sea-lions. As long as the sea-lions are above the tide mark they are relatively safe.**

deeper water right up to the beach. Sea-lions basking in this spot are closer to the open sea than they realise. From time to time, all year round, killer whales charge up the gully and on to the beach, diving headlong amongst the sea-lions until they can grab one in their teeth. Turning back to the sea, each whale humps itself along like some huge maggot until a wave lifts it clear of the bottom, and it swims free.

The best time of year for this style of hunting is in March, the southern autumn. This is when sea-lion pups start to adventure into the sea. At Punta Norte the whales take larger prey too. On the same beach, a small colony of elephant seals breed. Year-old males are just beginning the endless struggle for seniority which will absorb them every breeding season. Tussling at the water's edge, they sometimes fail to notice the patrolling killer whales, or to be aware of their own, perilous position on the beach. Three or four times a day, the whales visit the beach to probe the gully with their echo-location. When they detect the bulk of a half-tonne (1,100lb) elephant seal in the surf, the whales' attack is swift, accurate and often successful.

Overleaf **Killer whales use sonar to find their prey and to navigate through coastal inlets and bays. They also have a range of contact calls, clicks and whistles. No one knows the meanings of these sounds but each pod has its own distinct dialect.**

Above and right **The killer whales that live around Peninsula Valdes in Argentina have learned how to beach themselves and snatch sea-lion pups from the shore. The pups often seem oblivious to the danger. Often the first they know of the whale's presence is the huge bow wave that engulfs them an instant before the whale itself. The best time to hunt sea-lion pups is when they first start to leave the safety of the beach and learn to swim. However, although whales do kill them in the open sea, they much prefer to hunt them at the water's edge.**

Killers in Captivity

The change in attitude towards killers may have started in a small way with Moby Doll, but it became permanent later in the 1960s with the opening of dolphinaria featuring displays by killer whales. Millions of holiday makers in the United States included a visit to such a honeypot in their itinerary, along with Disneyland and the battlefields of the Civil War. After watching the seals being fed and gazing wide-eyed as sharks circled in a giant tank, the family could take their seats in a grandstand to see the killers. Music swelled, glamorous trainers leapt on to podia, and with a mighty splash two or three gigantic whales broke surface in a perfectly synchronised show of leaps and tail-wagging. These killer whales were stars, beautiful and dramatic, portrayed as having a sense of humour as they swept gallons of water over the crowd, or leapt from the water carrying their trainers on their nose.

For many years, these displays were accepted as a way of raising public consciousness about whales, at a time when whales needed all the support they could get. The captive killers were referred to as 'ambassadors for their species', as if they had submitted voluntarily to being held captive. There is no doubt that they were very effective at changing people's attitudes, and that they made a great deal of money for their captors. For many people, this was the first and only time that they would see a live killer whale. Most pronounced the experience moving, saying that it had altered their perception of whales in general and killers in particular.

However, killer whales do not adapt well to captivity. Of the 127 wild killers that have been taken into captivity since 1961, only 35 of them are still alive. The average life expectancy of a killer whale after it has been captured is little more than ten years, compared to up to seventy or eighty years in the wild. Gradually, the sympathy of the public shifted: from being amazed that the whales were gentle, not murderous, people began to ask whether they might be worthy of better treatment. Was it right to hold in captivity an animal that is now believed to be so intelligent?

*Right **Performing killer whales introduced many people to the wonder of these magnificent creatures, but the early deaths of the captive animals are a clue to the suffering they must endure.***

The trainers were among the first to realise that the whales in their care were deteriorating, both physically and mentally. Males developed a collapsed dorsal fin, only rarely seen in the wild, and generally accepted as a sign of poor condition. Worse than that, the behaviour of the whales began to change.

The earliest whale-keepers were amazed by the docility and intelligence of the animals in their charge. There is a famous story told by one of the Canadian trainers, Paul Spong, of the day when he was sitting with his feet in the water of the pool as a whale approached. His instinct was to withdraw his feet, but the whale was too quick for him. Taking his feet firmly in its teeth, the whale hovered in the water, holding Spong immobile but taking no other action. Eventually, it released the trembling man, leaving him with the lasting impression that the whale was fully aware of its power, but bore him no ill will.

Significantly, Spong was one of the first trainers to leave the dolphinarium business, setting up a whale-watching station off the east coast of Vancouver Island, where he devotes his time to the study and protection of wild whales.

Other trainers shared his experience of the generally trustworthy nature of killer whales in captivity. They described them as being like big dogs, playful, even humorous, enjoying the company of humans. Then a series of 'accidents' culminated in a trainer being drowned by three whales acting together, something everyone had said could never happen. This made people wonder whether the captives were going insane. If it can happen to captive primates and polar bears, why not to whales ?

There may well be something in this. No one stopped to consider the effect on a captive whale of living in a pool, no matter how large, in which the walls were covered with smooth ceramic tiles. It seems to have escaped notice that the whale's world is largely defined by sound. Every call a captive whale makes must echo from the sides of its enclosure, until it probably feels as though it is living in a hall of highly reflective mirrors. Even with the best treatment in the world, the captive may be suffering extreme mental torment.

Considerations such as these have given rise to a growing movement against keeping killer whales in captivity. The smaller dolphinaria have

GABY: FREE THE STAR OF FREE WILLY

Kaiko, the star of the movie *Free Willy*, is apparently a very laid-back chap. His attitude to life is probably one of the main reasons he is still alive today.

There is strong evidence that stress is the primary cause of death in captive orcas. In the wild, males are thought to live to between thirty and forty years old. In dolphinaria most of them die before they reach ten years of age. Kaiko is now nineteen. Only two males have lived longer in captivity. One died at twenty-three and the other at twenty-six years of age. It looks as though time is running out for our favourite killer.

The bad news is that he is still in his relatively small tank in Mexico. He is still performing, continues to suffer from a skin complaint and is worryingly underweight. Even worse, he now has five, instead of one, bottle-nosed dolphins in his already seriously cramped pool.

The good news, and it is great news, is that there is, at long last, a signed, twenty-five-page document detailing plans to move, rehabilitate and if possible, eventually free Kaiko. Four million dollars have been raised to pay for the project: two million from Warner Brothers and the other two from a private source. Well done all you kids who cared and wrote letters of complaint. Your support has been crucial in help-ing whale conservation groups world-wide fight for better conditions, including release, for all confined orcas.

And it's not just Kaiko. There are plans to release other orcas, including Lolita. She is the second-oldest female alive in captivity today. She is also the last of seven young whales captured from the southern community and sold to marine parks in 1970. It was the southern community that I saw, was filmed with, and came close to, so I would be particularly thrilled to see Lolita returned to the wild. Many of her older relatives that were allowed to escape but were photographed during the capture are still alive. Lolita was about 4.25m (14ft) long and seven years old when she was taken from the wild. She is now thirty-one, still a young female, in good health and an excellent candidate for release. Negotiations with her owners to establish a two-way link between Lolita and her pod in the sea are on-going. The intensity of the variety and quality of vocalisations between captive Lolita and her wild relatives would show just how much killer whales remember and recognise each other.

Hopefully, Kaiko should be moved in a few months' time to a specially built, spacious pool in New Port, Oregon. He will probably spend a year there to acclimatise to cooler water temperatures and a change of environment. He will also need to get fit before he can return to the ocean again.

In the meantime, Ken Balcombe and his team from the Center For Whale Research in the San Juan Islands have the task of locating Kaiko's family. Whales have large brains, so why not long memories? Many scientists are convinced that a family of killer whales will recognise a long-lost relative. Females can live to eighty, so Kaiko's mother and grandmother could still be alive. Then there are his aunts, uncles and cousins. Even if his family do not recognise him by sight, they should know that he is one of them by his dialect.

Kaiko was captured off Iceland. To identify his family, the research team will try to record the dialects of all the local groups, then compare them with Kaiko's. Ken and his team also hope to take skin samples for DNA fingerprinting. Modern technology is now so advanced that scientists can tell by looking at DNA (the information in our genes) whether animals are related or not.

Once Kaiko's family have been located, the plan is to take him, if he is fit enough, to Eskifjordur, a fjord in south-east Iceland.

When he has settled down there, acclimatised to the temperatures and can catch his own food, he will finally be reintroduced to his family. When that day comes, there will be millions of ecstatic children all over the world.

been forced out of business often simply because their whales died, and the larger have experienced a loss of public support. The 'Free Willy' story shows the depth of public feeling on the matter. Whale-watching in the wild is now a growing business, with boat trips and shore-based observation points all along the west coast of North America. The days of the dolphinaria may be nearly over, at least as far as their displays of killer whales are concerned.

The Story of Keet

Among the Native Americans of the Pacific north-west, the killer whale is held in deep respect. One clan in particular, from Vancouver Island, takes the killer as its totem, regarding it as protector and guide in this life and in the spirit world hereafter. They have a collection of legends portraying the killer as the father of the tribe or as a regular visitor to land, reporting to the tribe's ancestors on the progress and behaviour of their descendants.

Above **Killer whales often feature on totem poles. Many Native Americans, particularly those living on the north-west coast, revere killers and believe that the spirits of their ancestors live on in the whales.**

One killer-whale legend, the story of Keet, comes from the same area. It is often represented on totem poles, where the story starts at the top and moves down to its climax at the bottom of the pole.

Once there lived a great and respected hunter, called Naatslanei. He delighted to go hunting with his three brothers-in-law, enjoying their companionship and sharing the proceeds of the hunt at the end of the day. However, the brothers were jealous of his success, and one day they decided to kill him. They tied him up, and left him on a reef far from shore to drown when the tide came in. The youngest of the three brothers hated to leave him there, but he was powerless to do anything to help, so Naatslanei was left awaiting his fate. The cold tide crept over the rocks, lapping his feet, and he resigned himself to death.

As he sat there, a loon (a duck-like diving bird) appeared, swimming easily on the sea. The loon took Naatslanei to a secret world, inside the reef, where there were many other people who had been saved by the spirits. They put him inside a magic bubble, so that he could drift safely ashore.

Once he was ashore, he sent for his wife, with a message to bring his tools to him in secret. As well as being a great hunter, Naatslanei was a skilled carver of wood and ivory. He carved an evil-looking monster, which he named Keet. When the monster came to life, he spoke to it.

'I have carved you to avenge a great wrong-doing. There will be three men in a canoe. Kill the two bad ones, but spare the youngest.'

Keet swam off into the ocean. He executed the two elder brothers, and swam back to shore with the youngest riding on his back. Naatslanei then ordered Keet never to harm humans again, and released him into the sea, to swim free for ever more.

187

6

Leopards and Cheetahs:

Dappled Predators

Lithe and beautiful, the two large spotted cats of Africa are similar at first sight, but very different in their way of life. Although both are solitary hunters, their techniques are quite distinct and they hunt most successfully on different terrain. The cheetah is a day-time sprinter, at home on the open, short-grass plains, while the leopard stalks its prey from cover, often at night. Both suffer from the attention of scavengers, principally lions and hyaenas, and both have particular reason to fear discovery by vultures.

Left **Once cheetahs ranged throughout the plains of Africa, the Arabian peninsula and as far east as India. Today there are precious few of them outside Kenya, Tanzania and Namibia.**

Fastest on Four Legs

A cheetah in full pursuit of its prey is a spectacular sight as it twists and turns at the head of a column of dust, finally tripping a gazelle from behind and strangling it with its jaws. The cheetah is renowned as the fastest four-legged animal, capable of sprinting at over 100km (62 miles) per hour for up to 400m (440yd). It hunts by sight, often surveying a herd of prey from a high vantage point before beginning the chase. It is wonderfully adapted for its way of hunting, from its jaws to the tip of its tail.

A cheetah has blunt claws, at the end of very long, slender legs. The claws cannot be retracted as much as those of other cats, acting instead like permanent running spikes to give it a grip on the dusty ground. The power they transmit comes partly from the powerful hindquarters, but also from the large muscles along the cheetah's flexible spine, which make up a good proportion of the animal's weight of around 45kg (100lb). The bending and stretching of this long back is the secret of the cheetah's acceleration.

Running at this speed is inherently unstable, so the cheetah needs its long tail, heavy at the tip, to maintain its balance, especially when it turns to follow the jinking run of a gazelle.

Once it catches up with its prey, the cheetah trips it, using a dew-claw that grows, clear of the ground, on the inside of each front leg. Its next move in the hunt is crucial: gazelles have sharp little hooves, which could cause injury. The cheetah must grip the throat of its prey before it has time to kick, and hang on until the victim dies. The cheetah's short jaws are not very powerful, but they are enough to shut off the windpipe of its panting prey, though its grip rarely even breaks the skin, let alone the neck. It has especially wide nostrils, so that it can pant effectively with its mouth closed, while it strangles the gazelle.

The range of prey taken by cheetahs is surprisingly limited. Some animals are simply too big to be overpowered: giraffe, eland and buffalo are beyond a cheetah's capabilities. Some are too agile, such as the nimble little dik-dik, and some too fierce and dangerous to attack, such as adult warthogs and troops of baboons. But there are others that would seem

Right **The cheetah is a fussy eater. It will eat only fresh meat that it has killed itself. Its favourite prey are small antelope, such as Thomson's gazelle, springbok and impala.**

ideal in size and speed for such a rapid hunter. Vervet monkeys and bush hyrax are abundant and often come down from the trees, but the cheetah ignores them, as it does birds and snakes, and all small creatures. In the Serengeti, in Tanzania, it feeds almost exclusively on Thomson's gazelles, which are relatively common.

This selective hunting is the result of a simple equation: smaller prey would take more energy to catch than they would produce when the cheetah ate them. Thomson's gazelles are plentiful in the right habitat, relatively easy to catch, and nourishing enough to leave the cheetah's energy balance in profit. The distribution of cheetahs in the Serengeti is determined by the distribution of these small gazelles. Elsewhere in Africa, it feeds on other antelope of the same size, up to about 60kg (130lb) in weight. In South Africa and Namibia, impala fit the bill, while in Zambia, puku are the right size, and easy enough to catch.

Before a cheetah can hunt, its prey must flee. Male gazelles determined to hold a territory against other males sometimes refuse to run, leaving the cheetah baffled. If the gazelles stand their ground, the cheetah will walk away, looking for something that will 'play the game'. In one encounter that was filmed, three young male cheetahs approached two male Grant's gazelles, their horns locked in combat. The gazelles were too preoccupied to notice the cheetahs coming, and would have escaped attack if they had not suddenly looked up and panicked. As soon as the gazelles started to run away the cheetahs gave chase and eventually killed one of them.

Leopards do not select their prey in the same way as cheetahs. They will take all sizes, from the largest to the smallest, and also scavenge from any rotting carcass they might come across, while cheetahs will eat only prey they have killed themselves.

Above **The cheetah is the fastest animal on land. It can sprint at up to 100km (62 miles) per hour, but only over short distances.**

Power in the Night

Cheetahs are restricted to open savannah woodland or open plains with short grass, but leopards can live in a much wider range of habitat, from desert to rainforest, and from mountainous areas to swamps near the coast. Typically, leopards live and hunt mainly in wooded country or savannah with plenty of trees to provide cover, vantage points and safe places to take their kill. Savannah antelope such as puku and impala are common prey, but when they hunt on the plains, they compete with cheetahs for Thomson's gazelle.

Leopards hunt mainly at dawn and dusk, but they are adaptable animals and will work through the night or during the day if they need to. When a predator starts to hunt it is not guaranteed success: in fact, it fails more often than it succeeds. One scientist who watched leopards hunting in the Serengeti saw only three successful kills in sixty-four attacks. Much of their prey is quite small, however, and failing to catch antelope need not mean that the leopard is going hungry. When a study was made of the remains of food found in leopard droppings, 35 per cent contained rodents,

Right **Like an alley cat, the leopard is a loner who lurks in the shadows and areas of dappled light.**

Below **Leopards are equipped with everything a supreme predator needs: keen senses, a lithe and athletic body, sharp claws and strong jaws. This one has killed a young giraffe.**

194

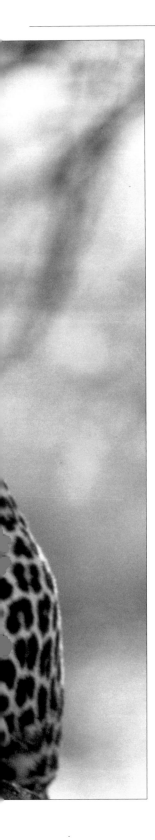

27 per cent birds, and 18 per cent the legs and wing-cases of insects. Such a diet does not lend itself to very dramatic hunting scenes. However, when larger prey is to be killed, the graceful leopard is wonderfully well equipped for the job.

By contrast with the cheetah's lightning dash, a leopard's methods are stealthy, relying on power in a brief final charge. A leopard weighs only about 15kg (33lb) more than a cheetah, but it will tackle young giraffe and buffalo, as well as picking off mice and small birds.

The home range of leopards can vary enormously in size. In Tsavo National Park, Kenya, they can vary from 9 to 63 sq km (3½ to 24 sq miles), each overlapping others, sometimes by as much as 70 per cent. The leopard patrols about half of its range regularly, and the rest less often, walking about 25km (15½ miles) every night while it is hunting. Leopards rarely rest in the same place on consecutive nights, unless they are mothers with small young.

A hunting leopard is the soul of patience. Crouched close to the ground, it will creep towards its prey a few centimetres or an inch at a time, using any cover there is, such as fallen branches or tufts of grass.

In national parks such as Luangwa, in Zambia, where visitors are taken on night drives to see the game, the resident leopards have been known to use the park vehicles as cover, not only hiding behind them, but using the noise and exhaust fumes to mask the sound of their movements and their scent. One particular female, known as Marmalade, regularly stalks her prey within arm's length of the astonished visitors. This presents a problem to the park staff. If their clients are to see anything, they must leave the vehicle lights on, but this dazzles the puku and impala which are the leopards' usual prey, making them easier to catch. If the lights are turned off, the leopard's job is only slightly more difficult: it can see better than the tourists, but the paying guests will see nothing of what happens. In general, the accepted rule is to avoid interfering with the natural course of events, so the guests miss the kill itself, but get a good view of the leopard feeding.

Left **The leopard's coat perfectly mimics the dappled light filtering through the trees where it rests, and under bushes in which it hides.**

At the slightest sign that its prey has detected it, the leopard will freeze, waiting for the prey to relax before it makes another move. Sometimes the stalking part of the hunt takes more than an hour, especially on a moonlit night when the prey is more than usually uneasy.

After its patient stalk, the leopard makes a short, but very violent charge to bring the hunt to an end. For its size and weight, it is probably the most efficient killer in all of Africa. It seizes its prey with flexible, needle-sharp claws, much more slender than those of the cheetah, and kills by biting into the skull or the neck, using its powerful jaws and long canine teeth. As a principally nocturnal hunter, a leopard has long sensitive whiskers, unlike the stubbly bristle on a cheetah's muzzle. The stocky, muscular

Right **The cheetah is the greyhound of the cat family, the ultimate feline athlete. Compared with a leopard, it is a delicate creature with the build of a fast sprinter.**

G ABY: C ATS' C LAWS

If you have ever played with a cat and accidentally had your hand hooked by one of its claws, you will know what lethal weapons feline talons are. The only way to extricate your hand without ripping skin is to wait for the cat to release you.

A cat's claws may be essential equipment for grabbing prey, but it has been suggested that they evolved instead for climbing trees. Hyenas, dogs, foxes and bears are mainly ground dwellers. When all these predators were evolving, it was an advantage for the cats to get up in the branches to hunt and hide. The use of claws as an efficient tool for holding down prey is thought to have developed later.

Cats have retractable claws. If they were extended at all times, they would become blunt like a

dog's. The cheetah is often described as having non-retractile claws. Some scientists now say that its claws are basically the same as other cats, they just cannot be withdrawn as far.

To keep their claws sharp and clean, cats rake tree trunks. The domestic variety have adapted to

Above **Cheetahs often use old termite mounds as vantage points, which made these animals easier for us to find than the more secretive leopard.**

using furniture as well, or instead, and have become adept at adding fringes, tassels and a certain 'shredded look' to loose covers and upholstery.

build of a leopard, with a powerful neck and broad head, gives it access to a much wider variety of prey. Leopards have been known to kill bull eland weighing 500kg (1,100lb), and there is a report of one killing an adult male gorilla four times its own weight.

Another difference between the leopard and the cheetah is persistence: if a cheetah misses its prey, it will give up the chase, exhausted, whereas a leopard will drop back into cover and wait for the herd to calm down before resuming the stalk.

The sheer power of a leopard is seen in what happens next: it carries its prey up a tree and wedges it among the branches. The prey often weighs as much as the leopard, or even more. There, it will be out of the reach of scavengers such as hyaenas and lions so that the leopard and its cubs can return to feed at leisure during the next few days.

A Family of Sprinters

The breeding season for cheetahs in the Serengeti starts in the wet months, from November to May, when they follow the Thomson's gazelle from the scattered woodlands out on to the open plains. Each female establishes a home range for herself, the biggest being more than 700 sq km (270 sq miles). These ranges are not exclusive but overlapping: because of the large area, the females rarely meet and competition is kept to a minimum. Each cheetah needs shade to rest in, plenty of gazelles to hunt, and a secure place in which to hide her young when they are born.

She will have as many as six cubs, covered during the first four months of life in soft greyish fur. She hides them in thickets of dense bush, guarding them at night, and returning to feed them between hunting trips during the day. Unlike the more versatile leopard, who can hide her young among masses of jumbled rocks or deep rambling gullies, the cheetah, being a creature of the open plains, must seek sanctuary in a limited range of rather obvious places. The cheetah's enemies can more easily pin-point where her young are hidden than they can with the much more elusive

Left A leopard's sharp and strong claws combined with its muscular body enable it climb high into the tree tops. It makes full use of this ability to cache its food out of the reach of lions, hyaenas and vultures.

leopard. Every time the female cheetah returns to her cubs, she is in danger of giving away the hiding place to passing predators, mainly lions and hyaenas, which will kill the cubs if they can find them. She approaches with great caution, alert for watching eyes. If she sees a lion in the area, she will turn aside and leave the cubs for a little while longer, until the lion goes away.

In spite of their mother's caution, cheetah cubs have a very small chance of surviving to adulthood. Nine out of ten of them die in their first three months: victims of grass fires, lions, hyaenas or simply starvation. A mother who can raise three cubs is doing very well; one or two is the usual number of survivors.

As soon as the cubs are strong enough, they join their mother in the hunt. At first, they may be more of a hindrance than a help, disturbing the prey before their mother is ready to begin her sprint, but gradually they become more competent and help to increase the amount of food the family can collect. When they are eighteen months old, they will leave their mother and set out on their own. The females from the litter go their separate ways, but the males will stay together for the rest of their lives.

All Boys Together

Being in a group of brothers is the best hope of survival for the male cheetahs. A male on his own cannot hold a territory for long and has little or no chance of breeding. Such solitaries, coming from litters in which they were the only male survivor, make up about 40 per cent of the male population. Half-starved, they spend their lives skulking in cover, trying to keep out of the way of large predators, including bands of other male cheetahs. If they are found they risk being killed in the deadly rivalry that precedes the mating season.

Although it is usually said that lions are the only big cats that live in groups, male cheetahs depend on the co-operation of their brothers for the

Right **Cheetah cubs follow their mothers out on to the open plains at about four months of age, but it can be a further fourteen months before they hunt on their own.**

Overleaf **It is an advantage for male cheetahs to form a coalition with their brothers. A team of males have a better chance of defending a territory against rivals than those on their own.**

rest of their lives. They hunt as a group, with difficulty at first, without their mother's leadership, often having to take desperate risks as they tackle unsuitable prey. Because they are in a group, they have more chance of success, even against antelope that are twice their weight, or warthogs that would be too dangerous for a single cheetah to tackle. When the time comes to breed, the band of brothers will mate as a group.

Two or three males together fight for and hold a territory, preferably at a place where several female home ranges overlap, so that they will have access to more than one mate. They mark the boundaries of the territory by leaving dung and sprays of urine on prominent landmarks, usually rocks and trees that are likely to be inspected by other passing cheetahs. The effect of this is to warn off other males, while the residents patrol their area regularly, keeping watch for females. The bigger the group of males, the better their chances of success: it has been found that two male cheetahs can hold a territory for about eight months, whereas three can hold a similar area for up to two years.

When the males find a female, they take it in turns to trail her until she comes into season. Again the advantages for the males of being in a group are plain. By taking turns, it is easier for two or three of them to trail a female until she comes into oestrus.

For the female, courtship appears to be a brutal affair, but in fact, this behaviour is important to trigger ovulation. When the female becomes receptive, the males all take part, chasing the female, growling and hitting

Left **The cheetah differs from the leopard in many ways. Its spots are small and uniform. It has longer legs, a more lithe body and smaller head.**

Right **Cheetahs regularly spray prominent landmarks in their territory with their urine. This warns rivals that the area is occupied and also leaves chemical messages that inform other cheetahs of the sex and reproductive condition of the owner.**

at her with their paws. Females in captivity that do not get this rough treatment are less likely to conceive. When the female becomes receptive, all the brothers usually mate with her. Only one of them will make her pregnant, but whichever it is, the result is a success, genetically speaking, because the family genes have been passed on.

Occasionally, male groups are made up of two or three solitaries of about the same age who have met and made friends during their time in the bush, as a means of self-defence against other roaming bands. About 20 per cent of male cheetah bands are of this sort. They co-operate in the same way as bands of brothers, though there is not the same genetic justification for it. They do not fight each other because, apart from the risk of injury, each member of the band needs his companions to be in good condition to fight off the challenges of other bands. In this respect, cheetahs behave very much like male lions in forming a team against rivals.

The Bottleneck

Cheetahs are notoriously hard to breed in captivity, and not just because the females lack the necessary bullying by a band of males to make them ovulate. The Indian potentate Akbar the Great was the first person to try to breed them, in 1555, from among his collection of 9,000 tame cheetahs with which he used to hunt gazelles. Out of all his animals, and with all the care that could be purchased with his wealth, Akbar succeeded in producing only one litter of three cubs. It was not until 401 years later, in 1956, that cheetahs were next bred in captivity, at Philadelphia Zoo in the United States. The feat was repeated many times after that, until by the end of the 1980s there were 200 captive-bred animals in the US. However, all was not well. Less than 15 per cent of cheetahs caught in the wild were breeding in captivity, and 40 per cent of their cubs died soon after birth.

For a long time, scientists found it hard to understand why cheetahs are apparently such sickly animals. Even in the wild, they are prone to genetic disorders such as malformations, and their cubs are vulnerable to a number of diseases, especially infectious peritonitis. All cats can catch this virus, but in all other species the death rate is about 1 per cent; in cheetahs it is more than 50 per cent.

Left **Young cheetahs recognise potential food according to what their mother brings them. As they grow older she allows them to play with live prey.**

A species' defence against disease is in the diversity of the immune systems of its members, produced by the mixture of genes that results from different individuals coming together in normal mating. Cheetahs evidently lack this diversity. Furthermore, males often produce abnormal sperm, and many of them show very low fertility.

When DNA testing became possible, scientists discovered that all cheetahs share a very large number of genes, with very little variation between individuals, in the same way as animals that have become inbred, that is, mated with close relatives. Inbreeding would produce just the same weaknesses in the stock as they had observed in cheetahs. The variation in the genes of today's cheetahs is the same as it would be if they were all descended from a single litter about 10,000 years ago.

This figure gave the scientists an idea. Between 10,000 and 12,000 years ago, during the last Ice Age, about 75 per cent of all large mammals died out. The researchers suggested that cheetahs may have been harder hit than some other large mammals, so only half a dozen of them survived, in some sheltered spot, to breed and give rise to the 20,000 or so alive today. This genetic bottleneck gave rise to the apparent inbreeding that is now apparent in cheetahs. All the usual mechanisms to prevent inbreeding are found in cheetah behaviour. The males leave the litter to go off on their own, splitting off from their mothers and sisters, for example; but because they are descended from such a small group of animals, they have no choice but to breed with close relatives.

Daylight Robbery and Theft in the Night

The family lives of leopards and cheetahs have a lot in common. The mothers of both species are single parents, having no support from the male, and both are therefore very vulnerable to scavengers, because they are reluctant to fight for their prey when another animal wants to steal it.

For cheetahs hunting in daylight, vultures are very bad news. They can spot a kill from a long way away, and they spiral down to it, gathering on nearby trees to wait for the predator to finish feeding so that they can come down and take their share. They do not drive off predators themselves, but they are the cause of other scavengers finding the site of the kill. Lions and hyaenas can see the movements of vultures from far away, and they are quick to put two and two together. They make for the place as fast as they can. If they find that the predator is a cheetah, they will have a feed with no further trouble.

Leopards, jackals and even baboons can drive a cheetah from her kill, even when she is accompanied by three grown cubs. None of them dares

Below **The advantage of male cheetahs teaming up is to hold a territory, but it also means that they have to share their kills. Squabbles over food are kept to a minimum and rarely go beyond a harmless snarl.**

risk a wound to a leg or a shoulder that might result from a fight: they are such finely balanced athletes that they might starve before they were recovered enough to hunt again. Groups of brother cheetahs are no more tenacious of their prey. All a cheetah can do is drag its prey under cover as soon as possible and eat it as fast as it can, before something else comes along to rob it.

As we saw in Chapter 3 on hyaenas, leopards also suffer from scavengers at night, especially in places like Luangwa National Park where hyaenas are so numerous. They have been known to hold their own against lesser challengers, but only if they can drive them away by threats. If the confrontation comes to the point of physical contact, the leopard will always withdraw. It is safer for it to go and hunt again than to risk potentially disabling injury. In one incident, reported by Richard Leakey, the celebrated anthropologist, a leopard attacked and drove off some hyaenas that were threatening her young. Even more unusual was the leopard that attacked a hyaena that had stolen a cheetah's kill, took the prey up a tree, and then came down to chase the hyaena away.

Above It All

A leopard, with its immense strength, has a defence against scavengers that a cheetah lacks. A mother leopard can drag her prey up a tree, where hyaenas and lions cannot follow, and leave it there for days, while she and her cubs feed. Without this ability to store food, cheetahs suffer.

Male leopards mate more cautiously than cheetahs, probably because they have to approach the female alone, not in a group, and the female is very strong and well armed. A male holds a territory that usually overlaps those of its neighbours, though there is a 'core area' from which intruders will be repelled. Females wander widely during the mating season, listening for the rasping or purring sound made by the resident male. When a female has found a male, she does not always respond immediately to his advances. It may take several days before she is ready to mate.

*Left **A leopard gives birth in a secluded spot: a clump of bushes, jumble of rocks, gully or cave. If the mother suspects her hiding place is in danger of being discovered, she will move the cubs, one by one, to a safer location.***

The cubs, usually two or three in number, are born blind, and are kept well hidden by their mother in crevices among rocks or in a hollow tree or sometimes in a disused aardvark's burrow. Their eyes open at six to ten days, and by the time they are six weeks old they are already beginning to eat solid food. At the age of three months they are weaned, but still depend on their mother to find their food.

While they are small, leopard cubs are sometimes killed by hyaenas and lions, but they are safer than cheetah cubs because they can climb trees and keep out of reach. Their mother takes them up into a large tree and leaves them there while she goes hunting.

At first, the mother brings food to the youngsters, but later she fetches or calls them when she has made a kill, showing them where she has cached it, up another tree. They follow her on longer and longer expeditions, learning to hunt and finding their way about the territory. The cubs hunt on their own between sharing meals with their mother, concentrating on smaller prey: this is presumably when they learn the nutritional value of beetles and rodents that will stand them in good stead for the rest of their lives, whenever food is short. This experimental period can be dangerous, because the cubs do not know instinctively what animals might be dangerous. A tussle with a puff adder, for example, might be the last mistake a cub makes: the snake's venom is quite powerful enough to kill a half-grown leopard.

Most cubs stay with their mother for nearly two years, before striking out on their own. Even then, they may still not be fully grown, but quite big enough to find their own food as they continue to mature.

The Human Factor

Both of the spotted cats have suffered from their contacts with humans. Cheetahs were once found all over Africa, across Arabia, north into the steppes and down into the Indian subcontinent. They have a very ancient association with people, who certainly robbed them of their prey during

Right **Leopard cubs spend hours playing. The activity tones their muscles and helps them to practise manoeuvres that will be essential for hunting and fighting when they reach adulthood.**

Above **Unlike leopards, cheetahs are poor climbers. They often use large boulders as a vantage point to survey their surroundings, look out for approaching prey and keep watch for lions and troublesome hyaenas.**

Left **As soon as they are strong enough, leopard cubs retreat to the safety of the tree tops while their mother is out hunting. Here they are out of the reach of enemies such as lions.**

hunter-gatherer times, and learned to use them to hunt with from a very early date. A silver vase, engraved with a picture of a cheetah wearing a collar, has been dated to 2300 BC. They must have been easy to catch by men on horseback because they tire so quickly. Once tamed they would make good hunting animals because they are used to being robbed of their prey and having to hunt again. Cheetahs were used for coursing in ancient Egypt, in the old Indian civilisations, and even in Italy up to the Renaissance. Many thousands of cheetahs must have been taken from the wild during the period when hunting with them was fashionable, but this was not the main cause of their vast reduction in numbers.

Much more prosaically, the cause of their downfall was sheep. Land suitable for gazelles is also good pasture for sheep, and as sheep herding spread across the cheetah's former range, it turned to mutton instead of venison as its staple diet. In the resulting confrontation with the shepherds, there could be only one winner, and the cheetah came off second best.

Below **The leopard has the widest range of any cat because it is the most adaptive. It can survive in grasslands, deserts, mountains, scrub, marshland and coastal areas because it will eat anything from worms to large antelope, berries to carrion.**

Leopards, too, have suffered a reduction in their numbers, though they still occur over a very wide area. All of Africa south of the Sahara, Arabia, India and most of the Far East still have at least relics of their leopard populations. There is a famous small group of leopards living at Ein Gedi, on the shores of the Dead Sea in Israel, which regularly raid the nearby kibbutz in search of cats and dogs to eat.

Like cheetahs, leopards have suffered at the hands of stock breeders. When their territory is taken over by humans, leopards are not frightened off like some other animals: they simply adjust their feeding habits to include whatever it is that the humans are breeding. After a brief period of plentiful food the conflict starts, and the leopards are the losers.

An aspect of leopard–human relationships that is not found where cheetahs are concerned is man-eating. It is not a regular occurrence, but

GABY: CHEETAH HUNT

It was our last day in Kenya. We had completed filming, but decided to make a last trip out on the plains just to savour the animals.

We headed for a nearby crossing place in the Mara River. Here huge crocodiles lie in wait for zebra and wildebeest, which come to drink or ford the river. When we arrived there was a small herd of zebra and Thomson's gazelles waiting nervously some distance from the water's edge. The animals all seem to sense the danger lurking in the depths and it can take them hours to pluck up the courage to quench their thirst.

As we sat quietly watching them we suddenly saw a female cheetah and her three nearly full-grown cubs rise like ghosts from the long grass. On some unseen signal, the three cubs froze on the spot. For the next thirty minutes they did not move a muscle. Their mother, in the meantime, stealthily circled the herds. We could not believe that we were about to witness a hunt.

The female's skill was incredible. She crept up on a group of gazelle and just when we were sure she was about to make final move, she amazed us by standing up so that she was in full view. Her prey fled instantly while she just stood there watching them. We were totally confused, until she suddenly sped to the right, moving the fleeing herds straight

at ther waiting sons. It was then that we realised that this was a training session.

What ensued was bedlam. There seemed to be cheetahs and antelopes running in all directions, jumping over each other and stirring up a huge cloud of dust. It seemed incredible to us that the young cheetahs failed to make a kill, but fail they did. It made me realise just how much a predator, like a cheetah, has to learn to be a successful hunter.

The female did not even seem annoyed, She simply stalked over to a mound and settled down for

Above **People are not allowed to get out of their vehicles in national parks for obvious safety reasons. But outside the park boundaries, and with the expert help of our camp manager, Jock Anderson, I was able to have a really close encounter with a family of cheetahs.**

a well-earned rest. When her sons joined her, she gave them all a good grooming and then promptly fell asleep. A couple of hours later, we heard that she had killed a Grant's gazelle but that it was almost immediately stolen by lions.

The episode showed me that life really is tough at the top.

Above **In comparison to the cheetah, the leopard is a muscular bruiser. It has a more powerful, heavier body and a wider face and head.**

Left **The cheetah's distinctive tear strips may be to accentuate its facial expressions, although some scientists believe they may be a practical form of reducing glare.**

there have been scattered outbreaks in various parts of Africa for as long as people have been there. Typically, the killings occur when people first spread into an area, while the leopards are adjusting to the change in available prey. The leopards are not the only culprits: lions also ocasionally eat people, until the inevitable happens and both species are persecuted until they learn to fear people, and keep out of their way.

A separate, and wholly despicable, cause of the decline in numbers of all the big cats is hunting for skins. The patterns and markings that evolved to make the leopard and the cheetah inconspicuous in the bush is stolen and sold to make a rich human stand out in a crowd. One sign that civilisation may actually be improving, albeit very slowly, is the massive decline in the fur trade as a result of public opinion.

Spots

The spotted coats of the leopard and the cheetah that have made the cats so popular with furriers are superficially similar, but different in their fine detail and in the way in which they aid the animal's camouflage.

The spots on a leopard's body are joined together in rosettes, to produce a pattern on a larger scale than the fine spots on a pale background that make up the cheetah's pattern. The leopard's mimics the dappled light and shade under bushes, where most of them spend the heat of the day. Lying motionless, a dozing leopard is practically invisible, especially on a bright day when the shadows look all the deeper. Passing prey are less likely to notice the leopard and take fright. The camouflage works well when the leopard is sitting high in a tree with light filtering through the leaves

A cheetah's camouflage may be more defensive than aggressive. It is most effective in shade, not while it is hunting in the open. This may be connected with the mother's need to be able to visit her cubs secretly, without attracting the attention of passing predators, as well as to rest in peace during the day. In the open, the lighter colour helps to conceal the cheetah against the dusty ground, but it is nothing like as effective as the golden camouflage of a lion, almost invisible among dry grass.

Some scientists have suggested that the black 'tear stripes' below a cheetah's eyes may be a way of reducing glare when it is following prey, rather as an American footballer paints his cheekbones black. Others suggest that the stripes emphasise the cheetah's facial expressions, which are certainly more varied than those of many other cats.

At one time the so-called 'king cheetah' was thought to be a separate race, with striking markings in which the spots are joined together into large blotches, but nowadays it is recognised merely as a mutant form.

The spotted skin of the leopard was honoured in early Africa, its use being granted only to warriors or, in some tribes, only to the king. In Buganda (an area of Uganda), according to Jonathan Kingdon, the fur from a leopard's tail is thought to have magical properties. Cut off and smoked in a pipe while the appropriate prayers are said, it is supposed to bring home a wandering wife or other relative. As the tail of the leopard is always restless, the saying goes, so may the wanderer's heart be uneasy until he or she returns home.

Right **Over a hundred years ago, Gerard Manley Hopkins wrote a now-famous poem, Pied Beauty, that celebrated all things spotted and speckled; he spoke of 'stippled trout' and 'finches' wings'. Perhaps he never saw a cheetah or a leopard, for they would surely figure in a poem that begins 'Glory be to God for dappled things...'**

Acknowledgements

While on location in America and Africa, filming the Survival Predators series, everyone in the crew experienced moments of fear, suffered from sickness, sunburn, swarms of mosquitos, unbelievably irritating tsetse flies, frustration, the cold and the heat. However, these irritations pale into insignificance when compared with the hours of pure joy, exhilaration and exuberance that we shared.

I would like to thank Survival's editorial, production and library teams who worked long hours back at base and pulled out the stops when necessary to ensure everything stayed on schedule; everyone who assisted us on location, without whose expert help we could not have captured on film many special scenes; the crew, who cheerfully kept going, sometimes late into the night and after repeated 4.30am wake-up calls; Clem Vallance, our director, for his experienced guidance and for keeping a cool head under pressure; Malcolm, my co-writer, for his expertise and hard work; and last but not least, Gaby, for being such a sport, for her endless enthusiasm, infectious energy, support and friendship.

Caroline Brett

Photograph Acknowledgements

The authors and publisher would like to thank the following for the use of their photographs in this book: Ken Balcomb 155; 158; 161; 166   Des & Jen Bartlett/Survival Anglia 17; 23; 37; 38; 39; 46; 176; 178; 188; 191; 199; 208   Joel Bennett/Survival Anglia 124; 126; 130; 142; 147   Joe B Blossom/Survival Anglia 63; 107   Caroline Brett/Survival Anglia 2-3; 6; 7; 8; 9; 32; 44-5; 53; 66; 103; 135; 136; 143; 156; 162-3; 173 (top and bottom); 186; 198; 219   Bob Campbell/Survival Anglia 22; 104; 116; 117   Daniel J Cox/Oxford Scientific Films 187   Deeble/Stone/Survival Anglia 18; 92; 195; 196; 200; 203; 215; 216; 218   Jeff Foott/Survival Anglia 51; 123; 131; 133; 134; 138; 141; 144; 149; 150; 152; 164; 165; 168; 170; 180; 181; 181 (top) 223   Nick Gordon/Survival Anglia 57; 67   Robert Harvey/Survival Anglia 60-1   Mike Hill/Oxford Scientific Films 183   Paul Johnson/Survival Anglia 24   Richard & Julia Kemp/Survival Anglia 76   Chris Knights/Survival Anglia 204   Mike Linley/Survival Anglia 52; 69; 75 (top and bottom)   Matthews/Purdy/Survival Anglia 12; 20; 26-7; 28; 29; 30; 33; 34-5; 40; 42-3; 79; 82; 85; 86; 88; 94; 99; 100; 102; 106; 112; 114; 217   R L Matthews/Survival Anglia 84   John Pearson/Survival Anglia 85 (top); 90; 91; 110; 111   Malcolm Penny/Survival Anglia 128; 129; 140   G D Plage/Survival Anglia 207; 211   Dieter & Mary Plage/Survival Anglia 10; 212; 221   Mary Plage/Survival Anglia 220   Mike Price/Survival Anglia 54   Rick Price/Survival Anglia 118; 148   Alan Root/Survival Anglia 48; 55; 68; 77; 78; 81; 97; 206   Joan Root/Survival Anglia 15   D M Shale/Oxford Scientific Films 174   Vivek Sinha/Survival Anglia 56; 64; 195   Claude Steelman/Survival Anglia 14; 58; 70; 73; 121   Janeen R Walker/Survival Anglia 192   Colin Willock/Survival Anglia 108